MW00626700

OPAQUE GLASS

S. T. Millard

Copyright © 1975
Wallace-Homestead Book Company

ISBN: 0-87069-130-9

Photographs by C. J. Boeger, Topeka, Kansas

Published by
Wallace-Homestead Book Company
P. O. Box BI
Des Moines, Iowa 50304

Printed in U.S. A.

Opaque Glass

A book showing a major portion of Opaque Glass in their various forms. A nomenclature is here promulgated with a view to making uniform the vast production of this type of glass.

By
S. T. MILLARD

FOURTH EDITION

OPAQUE GLASS FOREWORD

Originally published in 1953, OPAQUE GLASS by the late Dr. S. T. Millard was universally regarded as the basic reference on milk glass by antique collectors and dealers alike.

For over fifteen years, OPAQUE GLASS has been out of print and available only at premium prices on the rare book market. Now, thanks to the offset method of printing, WALLACE-HOMESTEAD has made this new edition of OPAQUE GLASS available again at a reasonable price.

The original plates for OPAQUE GLASS were destroyed many years ago so this volume was reproduced from an original copy supplied to us by Dr. Millard's daughter, Arlyne Millard Shortt.

It is a tribute to Dr. Millard's work that OPAQUE GLASS is now available to a whole new generation of collectors.

Acknowledgements

Gratitude is here expressed to those many loyal friends who have contributed small numbers of their splendid peices of glass for photographs. It is impossible, with the space alloted this subject, to mention them all specifically, but it is hoped they will accept my deep appreciation for their friendly and valuable contributions. There are several, who by their extensive and valuable contributions, must be mentioned specifically. I am greatly indebted to Mrs. Alexander Janssen of Kansas City, Mo.; to Mrs. B. H. Wheeler of Kansas City, Mo.; to Mrs. Nellie Vilm of The Victory Junction Antique Shop; to Philip Wirtsch of Kansas City, Mo.; To Donald's of Kansas City, Mo.; to Dr. Frank Patterson of Hunter, Okla.; to Mrs. Hazel Dall of Garber, Okla.: to Mr. Wallace Eaton of Charleston, Ill.; to Mr. W. L. Emmons of Jacksonville, Ill.; to Mrs. Bess Wilson of Rockford, Ill.; to Mrs. J. S. Collins of Topeka, Kans.; to Mrs. A. W. Smith of Garfield, Kans.; to.Mrs. L. N. Lindsey of Forsyth, Ill; to Mr. Don Rollins of Grand Ridge, Ill.; to Mrs. Janet W. Hirsch of Chicago, Ill.; to Mrs. Wilkerson of South Kansas City, Mo.; to Mr. J. E. Nevil of Cincinnati, Ohio; to Dudgeon's Antique Shop of Pittsburg, Kans.; to Mr. Powell of Topeka, Kans.; to Mrs. W. T. Ferguson of St. Louis, Mo.; to Mrs. Leona Glitsch of Oklahoma City, Okla.; to Mrs. Hinkle Guy of Topeka, Kans.; to Mrs. Nora Swords of Topeka, Kans.; to Mrs. Robert F. Sloan of Des Moines, Ia.; to Mr. E. V. Noble of Cedar Rapids, Iowa.

SWAN TOUREEN

LARGE ROSE VASE

The Serenade   Arch Border

PLATE 1

Wicket Edge   Pansy and Chain, Square

PLATE 2

The Serenade—A handsome, small plate made in 6½ inch diameter only. It was created by the Indiana Tumbler And Goblet Company, at Greentown, Ind., and was in white only.

Arch Border—An attractive, open edge plate created by Challinor, Taylor & Co., of Tarentum, Pa., in 6, 8, 9 and 10¼ inches in diameter. It has been seen only in white. Often the surface appears dull due to the use of tin oxide in the mixture instead of cryolite.

Wicket Edge—A product of The Atterbury Co., of Pittsburg, Pa., during the 80's. It was made in white, blue, black and possibly nile green. It was made in round and square shapes and the sizes were 7, 7½, 8, 8½ and 9 inches..

Pansy And Chain, Square—This is a very unusual plate and attractive, but not many of them are found. It was created in white and blue, and the sizes encountered are 7 and 8 inches.

Forget-me-not, Triple Row—This particular plate shows a row of beads around the collar. It is a product of The Canton Glass Co., of Marion, Ind., and was made during the early 90's. It was made in white and blue. The sizes were 7, 8, and 9 inches.

Peg Border—This is a product of Challinor, Taylor & Co., and was made in round and square shapes. It comes in white, blue and black colors. The dimensions were 7, 8 and 9 inches.

Forget-me-not, Triple Row   Peg Border

PLATE 3

Backward "C"   PLATE 4   Key Hole Border

Angel Head   PLATE 5   Block Border

Backward "C"—A collector's piece which comes in white and blue. The sizes encountered are 7, 8, 8½ and 10 inches. It is round only.

Key Hole Border—So named because of the resemblance of the openings in the border. It comes in white and blue. The sizes met with are 6½, 8 and 9 inches. There may be black plates of this pattern but they were not seen.

Angel Head—A rather heavily made plate with angel heads serving to quarter the border surface. It comes in white and blue colors. The sizes are 7½, 8½ and 9 inches.

Block Border—A fairly deep plate with square blocks to form the openings in the border. It has been seen only in white and blue. The sizes encountered have been 7½, 8½ and 9 inches. It was made in round only.

Double Scroll Border—A plate with two rows of scrolls and a scalloped edge on the border. It has been seen in white only. It has been found in 7, 8 and 10 inches.

Stanchion Border—Here is an unusual plate by Challinor Taylor & Co., with marked opalescent surface. It is quartered by segments dipping to the collar. It was made in white and blue and possibly nile green. It has been found in 7, and 8½ inches only.

Double Scroll Border   Stanchion Border, Scalloped

PLATE 6

Pie Crust Border   Notched Block Border

PLATE 7

Square Block Border   Forget-me-not. Plain Yoke, Triple Row

PLATE 8

Pie Crust Border— A very unusual plate showing a fluted edge with yoke-like elements in octagon shape. It comes in white only. The dimensions found are 7, 8 and 9 inches.

Notched Block Border—This is another example of the block border but each block has well defined notches on the blocks and thus makes a variety. It is in blue and white. The sizes met with have been 7, 8¼ and 9 inches.

Square Block Border — Another variety of the block border, but in this case the blocks are small and square. It has been created in white and blue. The following dimensions have been met with, 7, 8¼ and 9 inches.

Forget-me-not, Triple Row—This is similar to a former cut shown but this plate shows a plain collar which flares out more than the former pattern shown. Was made by the Canton Glass Co., Marian, Ind., It is both blue and white and shows 7, 8, and 9 inch diameters. No beads around collar.

Spring Meets Winter—A rather wide border plate, showing scenes in a deep bowl. A very elaborate edge, made in white only. It is an 8 inch plate.

Club, Shell And Loop Border—A plate showing all the elements named in the border. There have been various types of this plate and various paintings on the bowl. They show the following sizes, 7¼, 8½, 9 and 9½ inches.

Spring Meets Winter   Club, Shell and Loop Border

PLATE 9

Triangular Leaf and Chain   PLATE 10   Heart Shaped

Lattice Edge   Columbus

PLATE 11

Triangular Leaf And Chain—A very attractive plate with an elaborate border. The three point leaves intertwined in the chain elements. This comes in white and blue. The sizes are 7½, 8 and 10 inches.

Heart Shaped—A very unusual type of plate and very ornamental. It was made by the Canton Glass Co., and is found in blue and white. It was made in 6, 8 and 10 inches.

Lattice Edge—A plate usually found with paintings in the center. They were created by The Atterbury Co., Pittsburg, Pa., during the 90's. They are found in blue and white. They were made in 8, 9 and 10 inches.

Columbus Plate—This plate shows and outline of the profile of Columbus raised slightly on the bowl. The edge is the club and shell variety, but without the open rings. It is a 9½ inch plate.

Club, Shell and Loop Border, Plain—This plate is similar to another shown but has a plain bowl. It is in white and blue. The dimensions are 7¼, 8½, 9 and 9½ inches.

Beaded Loop Indian Head—A very attractive plate showing three rows of beads in draped fashion around a raised indian head. It has only been seen in white. The sizes are 7½ and 8 inches.

Club, Shell & Loop. Plain   Beaded Loop, Indian Head

PLATE 12

Lace Edge   PLATE 13   Angel & Harp

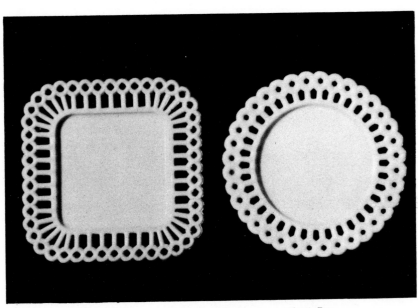

Square Peg   PLATE 14   Short Peg

Lacy Edge—A very pretty plate with definite lacy edge, and plain centre. It was made in blue and white. The sizes were 7½ and 8 inches.

Angel & Harp—A single row of Forget-me-nots around the border, and a raised angel holding a harp in arms, among the clouds, in the centre. It has been seen only in white. The dimension is 8 inches.

Square Peg—A desirable plate of the usual type border. It is made in white, blue and black. The sizes encountered have been 5, 7, 8¼ and 9 inches.

Short Peg—The usual type of this plate with the exception of having short pegs in the rim. It is found in blue and white. The dimensions are 5½, 7, 8 and 9 inches.

Fleur de Lis Border—An attractive plate often found with paintings in the centre and gilt or paint on the border. It comes only in white and is 7¼ inches in diameter.

Dart Edge—Here is a plate with an unusual border of dart like elements interspread with a series of notched figures. Blue and white. 7¼ inches in diameter.

Fleur de Lis Border   Dart Edge

PLATE 15

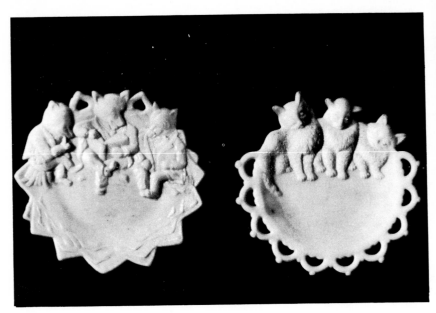

Three Bear   Three Kittens

PLATE 16

Rabbit Chariot   Cupid and Psyche

PLATE 17

Three Bear—An ornamental plate which comes in white and blue and was made in 7 inch diameter only.

Three Kittens—Another of the ornamental type of plates with a looped border. It was made in white and blue and was of 7 inch diameter.

Rabbit Chariot—An Easter plate with rabbits hitched to an egg chariot, driven by a chick. It was made in 7 inch diameter. "Easter Greetings"

Cupid And Psyche—A very ornamental type of plate with fancy border of a squarish nature. Was made in white only and is 7½ inches in diameter.

Easter Ducks—An Easter plate with four ducks in the centre and marked "Easter". It is 7½ inches in diameter, and white only.

Rooster And Hens—An Easter plate with a rooster and three hens. "No Easter without us." It was made in white only and is 7½ inches in diameter.

Easter Ducks   Rooster and Hens

PLATE 18

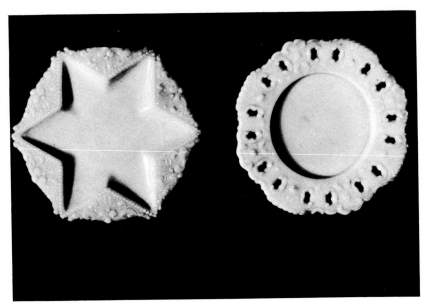

Star   Double "C"

PLATE 19

Scroll and Eye   Gothic

PLATE 20

Star—As the name indicates, a star shaped centre, with lacy edge. It was made in blue and white. It is 5½ inches in diameter.

Double "C"—A small plate with "C's" opposing each other in the border. A fairly deep bowl. Was made in white and blue. It is 6 and 8 inches in diameter.

Scroll And Eye—An attractive plate made by Atterbury Co. in the 80's. It was made in blue, white and black. The dimensions are 7¼, 8, 9 and 10 inches.

Gothic— A plate made by the Canton Glass Co. during the 90's and comes in white, blue and black. It was made in 5½, 7, 7¼, 8¼, 9 and 9¼ inches in diameter. Also Bryan, 9¼ inches in black.

Panelled Peg—An unusual peg type of plate with the pegs divided by a crown-like element. It was made in white and blue. The sizes made were 7¼ and 8 inches.

Three Owls—The usual ornamental plate with a looped border and three owls on the edge. It was made in white only. Diameter, 7 inches.

Panelled Peg   Three Owls

PLATE 21

Easters Chicks   PLATE 22   Chick and Eggs

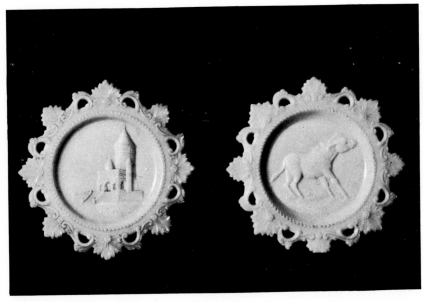

Ancient Castle   PLATE 23   Contrary Mule

Easter Chicks—Another squarish type of Easter plate with two chicks in the centre. It was made in white and blue. The diameter is 7 inches.

Chick And Eggs—A lacy edged plate with a chick and a basket of eggs near. "Easter Greeting." It was made in white and blue. The diameter was 7 inches.

Ancient Castle—The same type of border as in the last plate, but showing an old castle on the bowl. It was made in white and blue and is 7 inches in diameter.

Contrary Mule—The same type border as the former plate but with a mule pulling back on the leash. It was made in white only, and 7 inches in diameter.

Emerging Chick—A lacy edged, heart shaped border with a chick emerging from an egg shell. Comes in white and blue and was made in 7¼ inches in diameter.

Easter Rabbits—A scroll edge plate with two rabbits nibbling at the foliage in the centre. "Easter." Made in white only and 7¼ inches in diameter.

Emerging Chick   Easter Rabbits

PLATE 24

Club and Shell Border

PLATE 25

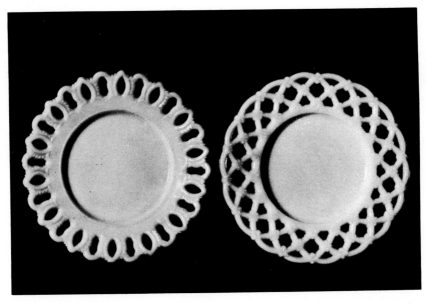

Leaf Edge

Deep Forget-me-not

PLATE 26

Club And Shell Border—A plate of the club type but the rings do not obtain in the edge. It is a Canton Glass Co. product. Comes in white and blue. The diameters are 7¼, 8½, 9 and 9½ inches.

101—A very attractive plate with the outline very definitely marked. It was made in white and blue. The diameters were 5, 7½, 8¼ and 9 inches.

Leaf Edge—A looped-like, open border with leaves overlapping the loops. It is found in white, black, and blue. The diameters were 5¼, 7¼, 8½ and 9 inches.

Deep Forget-me-not—A Canton product which shows a definitely deep bowl and no beads around the collar. It comes in white, blue and black. The diameters were 7, 8¼ and 9 inches.

Deep Lattice—An Atterbury product which shows a deep bowl and painted centre. It was made in white and blue. The diameters were 8 and 9 inches.

Pin Wheel, Painted—A shallow plate of this well known design, but with painting in the centre. It was made in white and blue. The diameters were 7, 8 and 10 inches. Made by Challinor, Taylor & Co.

Deep Lattice

Pin Wheel, Painted

PLATE 27

Lacy Edge Indian   Anchor and Yacht

PLATE 28

Lady At The Well   Flower Border

PLATE 29

Lacy Edge Indian—Another of the lacy edged plates with an Indian head in the centre. "Fort Necessity." The figure is raised above the surface. It comes in white only and is 7¼ inches in diameter.

Anchor And Yacht—A plate with an anchor and chain border and the yacht in the centre. It comes in white only and was 7¼ inches in diameter.

Lady At The Well—A very unusual shaped plate with a large scroll extending upward from the edge. There are two persons at the well. It was made only in white and 8¼ inches in diameter.

Flower Border—A very attractive plate with a deep bowl. The edge is a fine diamond weave with raised and painted flowers superimposed. It has only been seen in white. The diameter is 7½ inches.

Hare—A beaded edge plate with a comparatively large Hare sunken in the bowl. It has been seen only in white. It is 7½ inches in diameter.

Beaded Edge Dish—An elongated dish with a deep bowl which is plain except the large beads around the edge. Was made in white and blue.

Hare   Beaded Edge Dish

PLATE 30

Owl Lovers   Ring and Petal Border

PLATE 31

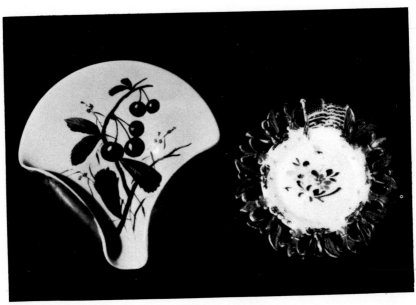

Crumb Plate   Fleur de Lis, Flag and Eagles

PLATE 32

Owl Lovers—An ornamental plate showing two owls in close contact on the Left, while a large parrot is on the Right. A 7 inch plate.

Ring And Petal Border—An unusual plate showing 7 elements in the petals with a ring between. The only size has been this 8 inch plate.

Crumb Plate—An old fashioned plate formerly used to gather up the crumbs from the table cloth. Cherries are painted in the centre. It is an 8½ inch plate.

Fleur de Lis, Flag And Eagles— A patriotic type of plate as indicated. They are usually found with gilt and colored paint on them. A 7 inch plate.

Down On The Farm—A large plate with farm scenes in raised figures and with a Roman key border. It has been seen only in the 10 inch size.

Roses And Poppies—A platter with small roses around the edge and poppies at either end. A very attractive piece and fairly heavy. It is in 7½ and 11 inches.

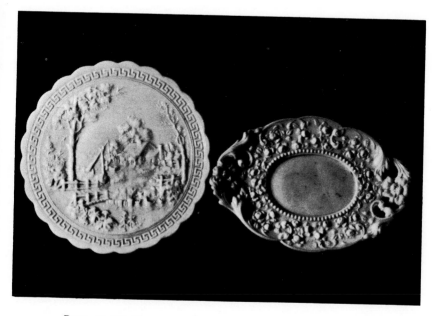

Down on the Farm   Roses and Poppies Platter

PLATE 33

Deep Pinwheel   PLATE 34   Heart Tray

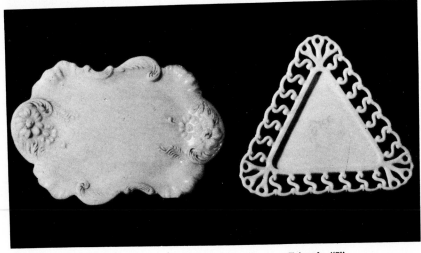

Sunflower Tray   PLATE 35   Triangle "S"

Deep Pinwheel—A plate with a deep bowl and the usual pinwheel border. It has been found in 7, 8 and 10 inches. Often is found painted in the centre. This piece shows a scalloped border beaded.

Heart Tray—A small dresser tray in the shape of a heart.

Sunflower Tray — An irregular, scroll type of tray with scrolls on the edge and sunflowers at each end. It is 10 inches long by 7 inches wide.

Triangle "S"—Just what firm made this plate is not certain. It is more ornamental than useful. It has been found in 7¾ and 8 inch sizes, rather scarce to pick up.

Rolled Edge With Pinks—A large bread or cake tray with edges rolled up and a spray of Pinks painted on the Centre. It is 10 inches square.

Cream Grape—A plate of this well known pattern, which is to be had in a full collection. The plate is 8 inches in diameter.

Rolled Edge With Pinks   Cream Grape

PLATE 36

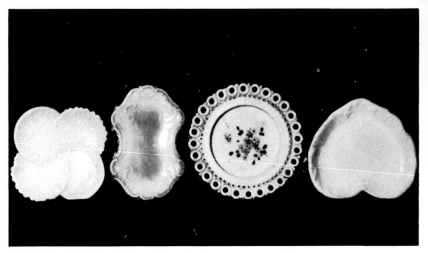

Scalloped Tray   Corset Tray   Ring and Dot Border   Shallow Heart Tray

PLATE 37

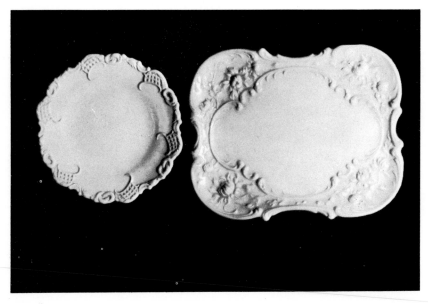

Scroll Edge   Dahlia Corner Tray

PLATE 38

Scalloped Tray—A 6 inch tray with four overlapping quarters which show ribbed surface and pansy-like elements. Blue.

Corset Tray—A small dresser tray resembling a corset in outline, which is 4 inches by 8 inches in diameter.

Ring And Dot Border—A small plate which is usually found painted on the bottom of the bowl. It is found in 5½, 7 and 8¼ inches.

Shallow Heart Tray—Another of the heart shaped trays with a shallow bowl and is 6 inches in diameter.

Scroll Edge—A handsome plate with scrolls around the border. It has been found 7 and 8 inches.

Dahlia Corner Tray—A large tray with Dahlias in each corner. It is attractive and useful for bread or cake or dresser. It is 8 inches by 10¼ inches in size.

Square Black "S"—An example of this well known pattern in the oqaque black. It has been found in 8 and 10 inch sizes.

Wicket, Black—The usual plate in this type but in the black oqaque color. It has been made in white, blue and black. The sizes met are 7, 8 and 9 inches in diameter.

Square "S" Black   Wicket, Black

PLATE 39

Black Leaf Border   Black, Square "S"   Stanchion Border, Black

PLATE 40

Stanchion Border, Blue   Battleship Maine, Blue

PLATE 41

Leaf Border, Black, Plate—A 7 inch plate of this well known pattern in the black glass. It is found in 7, 8½ and 9 inch.

Square "S" Plate, Black—Another black plate in the square "S" pattern. It is not so easily found. It comes in 7, 8¼, 9¼ and 10 inches.

Stanchion Border, Black, Plate— A black plate in this unusual type. It is found in 7 and 8½ inches only.

Stanchion Border Plate, Blue— Here is a stanchion plate in blue which is unusual to find. It comes 7 and 8½ inches only.

Battleship Maine, Blue, Plate—It is unusual to find this plate in blue with the ship painted in the centre. It is an 8 inch plate.

Anchor And Belaying Pin Plate— An unusual plate in that it shows a marked marine tendency. It has the belaying pins, rope, reeve eyes and anchor as a border. It has been seen only in white with the border painted. It is a 7 inch plate.

Lady Bust Platter—Here is an unusual platter of the rose and poppy pattern but with a Lady's bust in the centre. It has been claimed by some that this is the portrait of President Harrison's wife. I leave this for you to decide, it certainly favors her.

Anchor and Belaying Pin Plate   Lady Bust Platter

PLATE 42

Hen and Chickens   Rabbit and Horse-shoe

PLATE 43

Dogs and Cats   Negroes and Watermelon   Chick on Wooden Shoe

PLATE 44

Hen And Chickens—A lacy Edged Plate with "Easter Greetings", and a hen and flock of chickens in the centre. It was made in white and blue. The size was 7¼ inches.

Rabbit And Horse Shoe—Another decorative Easter Plate of 7½ inch diameter and was made in white and blue.

Dog And Cats—A lacy edged plate with a dog and two cas at the top. "He's All Right" inscription. It was made only in white and is a 6 inch plate.

Negroes And Watermelon—A half plate with two negroes and a hen eating on a slice of melon. It was made in white only and is a 7 inch plate.

Chick On Wooden Shoe—Another lacy edge plate in which the chick is riding the wooden shoe for a boat. It is a 6 inch plate. White only.

Green Leaf Plate—A small 6 inch plate allegedly for a tomato. It is of solid green color with raised leaves on the surface.

Waffle Centre—Here is another of the co-called club border plates with a waffle centre. It does not have the rings around the edge. It was made in white and blue. The sizes are 7 and 8¼ inches.

101—Here is a duplicate of another showing of this plate, but here shown to illustrate the small diameter found, this plate is 5½ inches.

Green Leaf Plate   Waffle Centre   101

PLATE 45

Yoked, Slatted Border   **PLATE 46**   Crown Border

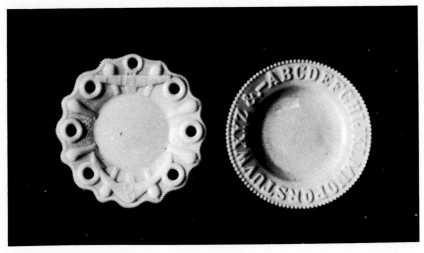

Marine Border   **PLATE 47**   A. B. C.

Yoked, Slatted Border—An attractive plate which comes in white only. The size is 7½ inches.

Crown Border—A rather lacy edged plate showing a crown tendency in the elements around the border. It was made in white only and comes in 7½ inch diameter.

Marine Border—A plate showing a series of belaying pins, reeve holes and a large anchor in the rim. It was made in white only and comes in 7 inch size.

A. B. C.—A plate with the alphabet around the rim in large letters. It comes in 7 inch size and should show blue color also.

Forget-me-not, S i n g l e Row—A plate with a single row of flowers around the edge and an open, lacy edge with beads around the collar. It was made in white and blue and comes in 7½ inch diameter.

"H" Border—Here is a plate of the same type as the "Wicket" but it will be noted there is no collar edge and the elements resemble the letter "H". A 7½ inch plate in white and blue .

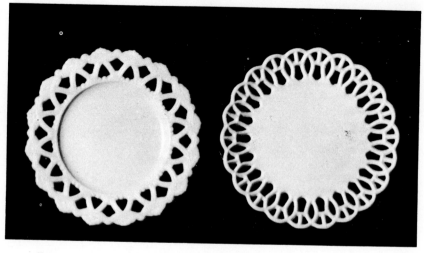

Forget-me-not, Single Row

"H" Border

PLATE 48

Leaf Edge Cake Salver   Beaded Edge Nappie

PLATE 49

Taft Plate   Bryan Plate

PLATE 50

Leaf Edge Cake Salver—A green leaf border salver of 12 inch diameter, and deep centre.

Beaded Edge Nappie—An attractive nappie of cream color with beaded edge. 8 inches in diameter.

Taft Plate—A campaign plate showing flags, eagles and stars around the border with profile of Taft in the centre. A 7 inch plate.

Bryan Plate—A campaign plate with a similar border to the mate on this cut, but showing profile of Bryan in the centre. A 7 inch plate.

Heart And Anchor—A very unusual plate showing alternating hearts and anchors around the edge, an 8 inch plate.

Lincoln Platter—An attractive platter with woven slatted edge and a highly raised profile of Abraham Lincoln in the centre. It is 8 by 10½ inches.

Heart And Anchor   Lincoln Platter

PLATE 51

Rock Of Ages   The Three Graces

PLATE 52

Rib Edge Tray   Pentagon Border Tray

PLATE 53

Rock Of Ages—A large platter with milk white overlay in the centre, showing persons at the "Cross". It is an attractive piece and hard to find.

The Three Graces—Here is another large tray with overlay centre of milk white glass, showing Faith, Hope And Charity around the rim.

Rib Edge Tray—A long dresser tray with ribbed edges which have been painted, as many of this type of pieces have shown. It is 15 inches long.

Pentagon Border Tray—A small dresser tray with five curved segments in the outline. It is of a scroll type with raised figures on the surface.

Fish Tray—Here are two fish which overlap forming a tray for pickles or similar usage. There are four small knobs for feet upon which it rests, a shallow bowl for pickles. It is an Atterbury product, of the 70's.

Scroll And Poppies Tray—A small tray for use on the dresser, showing poppies in either end and a scroll edge. It has been seen in white and blue. It is 4 inches by 7 inches.

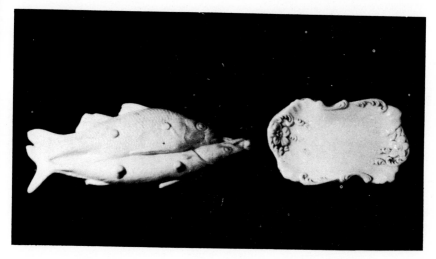

Fish Tray   Scroll And Poppies Tray

PLATE 54

Gargoyle Head Platter   **PLATE 55**   Plain Platter

Notched Platter   **PLATE 56**   Oblong Dresser Tray

Gargoyle Head Platter—A very attractive platter with gargoyles in each end and beaded centre. It measures 7½ by 11 inches in diameter.

Plain Platter — A heavy platter with deep bowl and ringed scrolls on each end. It measures 9¾ by 12¼ inches.

Notched Platter—A large platter with notched edges and measuring 9½ by 12¾ inches in diameter.

Oblong Dresser Tray—A long tray with irregular edges, measuring 5½ by 11 inches in diameter.

Three Monks, Ash Tray—A heavy tray with creases in the rim for cigar rests and showing the monks in the centre.

Ring Handled Tray—A scroll edge tray measuring 6 by 10½ inches in diameter.

Three Monks Ash Tray   Ring Handled Tray

PLATE 57

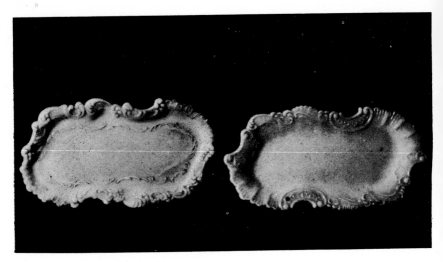

Oblong Scroll Tray   **PLATE 58**   Scroll Edge Tray

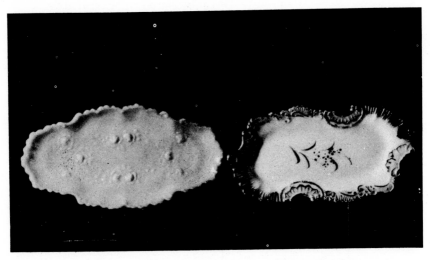

Wreath Dresser Tray   Ribbed Edge Tray

PLATE 59

Oblong Scroll Tray—Here is an irregular shaped scroll tray that measures 5½ by 9½ inches in diameter.

Scroll Edge Tray—Here is a tray that is somewhat similar to the one next to it but there is vast difference in the design viewed closely. It is of the same dimensions.

Wreath Dresser Tray—A rather light tray with wreath of roses in the bottom, it is 5 by 9 inches in diameter.

Rib Edged Tray—An irregular shaped tray with ribbed edges and painted, as is usual in many of this type of dish. It is 5 by 8½ inches in diameter.

Rolled Edge Tray—A rather heavy tray with rolled edges and narrowed sides. It measures 6 by 10 inches.

Question Mark Tray—A light tray with short scroll like elements on the surface and painted. It measures 4¼ by 8 inches in diameter.

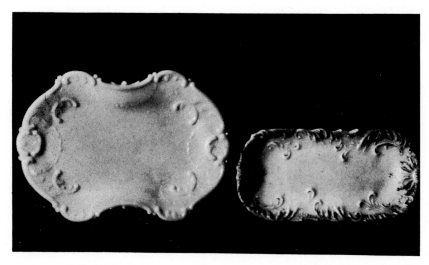

Rolled Edge Tray   Question Mark Tray

PLATE 60

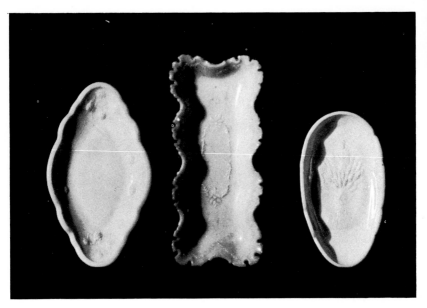

Pointed Tray   Scalloped Oblong Tray   Wheat Tray

PLATE 61

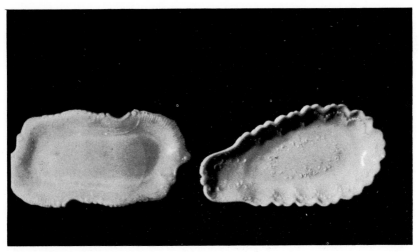

Scroll Whatnot   Scoop Tray

PLATE 62

Pointed Tray—A rather unusual tray with pointed ends and weak impressions in the bottom. It is 6 by 9 inches in diameter.

Scalloped, Oblong Tray—A long tray with scalloped border measuring 5 by 11 inches in diameter.

Wheat Tray—An oblong tray with a sheaf of wheat in the bottom, it is 4½ by 8 inches.

S c r o l l What-not—An irregular shaped tray with beaded border and notched edge. It is 6 by 8½ inches.

Scoop Tray—A peculiar scoop-like outline with scalloped border. It is 6 by 9 inches in diameter.

Retriever Platter—A large platter with a swimming dog in the centre. It measures 9¾ by 13¼ inches.

Beaded Edge Square Dish—A mate to a former piece shown measuring 5½ by 8½ inches in diameter.

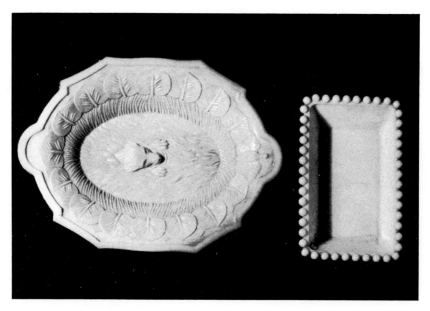

Retriever Platter   Beaded Edge Square Dish

PLATE 63

Ray End Tray   PLATE 64   Scalloped Edge Tray

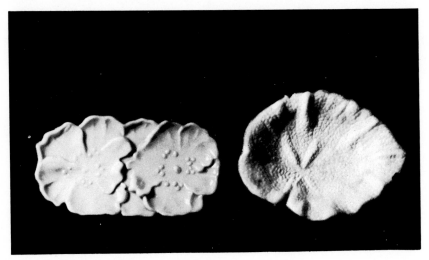

Pansy Tray   PLATE 65   Leaf Tray

Ray End Tray—A dresser tray with rays in each end and scrolls around the edge. It is 8 by 9½ inches.

Scalloped Edge Tray—A pretty dresser tray with wreath of small roses around the centre. It measures 7¾ by 9½ inches.

Pansy Tray—An unusual tray with three overlaping, large pansies. It is 4½ by 8¼ inches.

Leaf Tray—Another attractive tray with stippled surface and leaf veins over the surface. It is leaf shaped, 5½ by 7¼ inches.

Star Tray—A small star shaped tray with beaded edge. It is 5 inches in diameter.

Maple Leaf Nappie—A very pretty leaf shaped nappie with much veining on the surface. It is 5 by 7 inches in diameter.

Octagon Plate—A 7 inch plate of octagon outline and small scrolls around the edge.

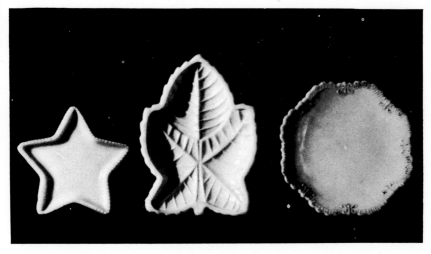

Star Tray   Maple Leaf Nappie   Octagon Plate

PLATE 66

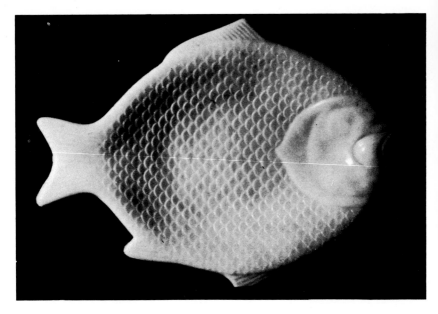

Fish Platter
PLATE 67

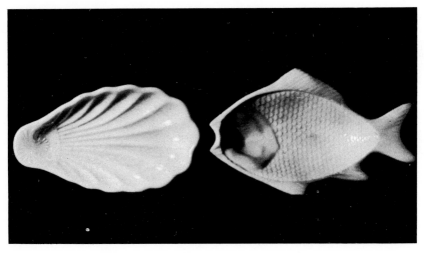

Shell Tray   Fish Pickle
PLATE 68

Fish Platter—A large platter in fish form, a product of The Atterbury Co., measuring 10 by 14½ inches.

Shell Tray—A shell shaped tray with shell ribs inside. It measures 5 by 8 inches in diameter.

Fish Pickle—Another Atterbury product in the shape of a small fish. It measures 5¼ by 8 inches. Made in the early 70's.

Hexagon Nappie—A scalloped edge nappie with ring handle. It is painted inside. It measures 8 inches across the scrolled edge.

American Skillet—A small skillet with the outline of both Americas in a figure resembling fried eggs, and a thermometer on the handle.

Grape Leaf Nappie—A notched edge nappie with grape design in the bowl. It is 6½ inches in diameter.

Hexagon Nappie   American Skillet   Grape Leaf Nappie

PLATE 69

Scroll And Eye Dish   Scroll Handled Tray

PLATE 70

Wreath, Footed Dish   Lace Edged Nappie

PLATE 71

Scroll And Eye Dish—A shallow dish of this pattern, made by The Atterbury Co., measuring 8 inches across.

Scroll Handled Tray—A tray with scalloped edge and scroll handles. It is 5½ by 8¼ inches.

Wreath, Footed, Dish—A shallow dish with flower wreaths around the bowl and scroll feet. It is 8 inches across.

Lacy Edged Nappie—A peculiar shaped nappie with rolled edges and alternate loops and petals on the edge. It is a 7½ inch nappie.

Draped Rib Bowl—A pretty bowl of 5¼ inches diameter and a draped like outline of ribs on the body and scalloped top.

Plain Bowl—A plain white tinged bowl measuring 5¼ inches in diameter.

Hob Nail Bowl—A small, 5 inch bowl with hobs on the major part of the bowl. It is modern.

Draped Rib Bowl   Plain Bowl   Hob Nail Bowl

PLATE 72

Beaded Rib Bowl   Square Lacy Edge Dish

PLATE 73

Lacy Edge Cake Salver   Crimped Edge Cake Salver

PLATE 74

Beaded Rib Bowl—A fluted bowl with beaded edge. It is 2¾ inches tall by 12½ inches wide and rests on a round foot. It comes in white and blue.

Square Lacy Edge Dish—An Atterbury product of the 80's and is 3¼ inches tall and 9¾ inches across the top. It has been seen only in white.

Lacy Edge Cake Salver—A salver with a two loop edge, which is 2¾ inches tall and 12 inches across the top. It is an Atterbury Product, also of the 80's.

Crimped Edge Cake Salver—As the name would indicate it shows a sort of crimped edge. It is an Atterbury production and is 11 inches across the top. It has been seen only in white.

Roman Cross Butter—A covered butter in this well known pattern. It is hard to find and brings a good price.

Barred Hobnail Sauce—A sauce measuring 4 inches across the top. It is a fairly modern piece but very much sought.

Barred Hobnail Compote—An 8 inch bowl to match the sauce beside it. They make a very desirable set.

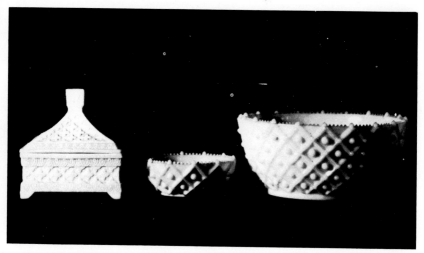

Roman Cross Butter   Barred Hobnail Sauce   Barred Hobnail Compote

PLATE 75

Looped Edge Dish   Hand And Dove

PLATE 76

Open Edge Beaded Rib Compote   Looped Edge Compote

PLATE 77

Looped Edge Dish—A lacy edge dish with loop elements and of an oblong shape. It was produced by Atterbury & Co. of Pittsburg, Pa. and it measures 5 inches tall by 9¾ inches long.

Hand And Dove—An oblong handled dish with lacy edge and on the cover is a dove held in a hand with a jewelled ring on a finger. It is an Atterbury Product and measures 4¾ by 8¾ inches.

Open Edge Beaded Rib Compote— A large compote measuring 11 inches across the top. It has fine beads on the rim and the lattice elements are slanting. The body is ribbed.

Looped Edge Compote—A very attractive, lacy edged compote with foot. The lace edge consists of two open loops. It is a product of The Atterbury Co., 12 inches wide.

Rolled Edge Nappie—A small dish or nappie with edges rolled up to make it appear square in outline. The edges are ribbed. It measures 8 inches across the top.

Pointed Lacy Edge Nappie—A very unusual shape and desirable. It has peculiarly pointed ends making it appear squarish. It is 11 inches across. An Atterbury Co. product.

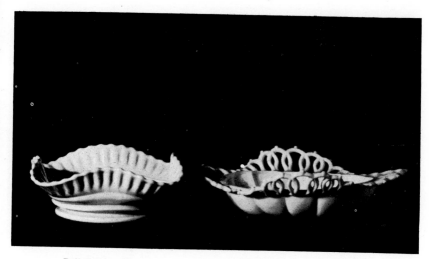

Rolled Edge Nappie   Pointed Lacy Edge Nappie

PLATE 78

Crossed Fern Compote and Sauces

PLATE 79

Notched Lacy Edge Nappie   Arch Border Compote

PLATE 80

Crossed Fern Compote And Sauces—A very attractive pattern. The compote measures 4 inches high and 8½ inches across while the sauces are 2½ inches tall by 4½ inches across.

Notched Lacy Edge Nappie—A pretty, shallow nappie with a heart and dot type of edge and measuring 8¼ inches across.

Arch Border Compote—A low dish or compote which is in blue and was made by Attérbury & Co., during the 80 s. It is 9½ inches across.

Panelled Flower Compote—Here is a very beautiful compote on a plate base. It is light yellow in color. It has stave like ends projecting above the edges. The plate is 9 inches in diameter while the bowl is 3¼ inches by 7½ inches across.

Lacy Edge Daisy Compote—A compote with raised figures of flowers and painted. A lacy edge adds to its beauty. It measures 4¼ inches high by 8¼ inches wide.

Panelled Flower Compote   Lacy Edge Daisy Compote

PLATE 81

Beaded Medallion Mug   Child And Dog Mug   Block And Jewel Mug
PLATE 82

Hobnail Bottle   Covered Hat   Pear Covered Dish
PLATE 83

Beaded Medallion Mug—A mug showing a portrait in a beaded medallion. It comes in white and blue.

Child And Dog Mug—A square handled mug showing a child and dog on the sides. It has been seen in white only.

Block And Jewel Mug—A fairly modern mug with the block and jewel band below on the bowl.

Hobnail Bottle—A modern bottle of this desirable pattern. It has a dark stopper which is hobbed.

Covered Hat—An unusual hat peice with a cover which has a knob on top.

Pear Covered Dish—A very attractive peice in the shape of a pear which rests in a petalled leaf bowl.

Hobnail Bowl, Pink Lined—A desirable piece in this pattern which is 8½ inches in diameter and is lined with red overlay.

Loop Edge Dish—A lacy edge dish with only one loop in the border. It is an Atterbury piece and measures 7¼ by 11 inches.

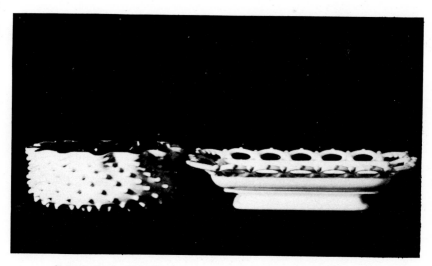

Hobnail Bowl, Pink Lined   Loop Edge Dish

PLATE 84

Teardrop And Tassel Sugar   Waffle Covered Sugar

PLATE 84—A

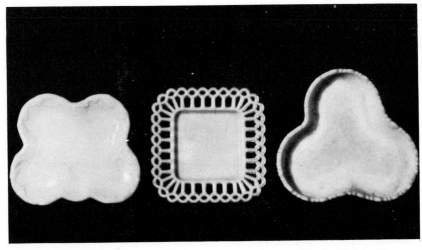

Five Loops Dresser Tray   Square Peg Plate   Triangle Dresser Tray

PLATE 84—B

Teardrop And Tassel Sugar—A rare piece of this well known pattern. It probably was made from the same molds as the crystal glass pieces. It is a pattern of the 70's. It comes in clear, blue and white.

Waffle Covered Sugar—A very pretty piece of this pattern and is hard to find in the white. It is a product of the 60's and is getting scarce.

Five Loops Dresser Tray—An unusual shaped tray in the white with fine scroll-like elements around the edge.

Square Peg Plate, Small—This is a duplicate of other plates in this pattern and is shown here to depict the small plate only.

Triangle Dresser Tray—An example of a dresser tray, which are common, in the triangle form.

Barber Bay Rum Bottle—A bulb bottom bottle with slender neck, for Bay Rum.

Ringed Vase—A short, squarish vase with two rings above and below on the body.

Bulging Vase—A vase with a large bulging base and a slender neck.

Carnation Vase—A tall, ruffled top vase with carnations painted on the body.

Barber Bay Rum   Ringed Vase   Bulging Vase   Carnation Vase
Bottle

PLATE 84—C

Thousand Eye Compote   Knobby Edge Compote

PLATE 85

Crinkled Lacy Edge Compote   'Scalloped Lacy Edge Compote

PLATE 86

Thousand Eye Compote—A very rare and unusual compote in blue. It is a product of Richards & Hartley of Tarentum, Pa. It measures 9 inches across the top.

Knobby Edge Compote—An unusual edge in its irregularity. It is an Atterbury product of the 80's, and is 10 inches across.

Crinkled Lacy Edge Compote—Another peculiar lacy edge and very desirable. It is an Atterbury production and was made during the 80's. It is 4 inches high and 7¾ inches wide at the top.

Scalloped Lacy Edge Compote—A dignified compote with a scalloped edge. It measures 3¼ inches high and 8½ inches wide.

Ball And Chain Edge Compote—A very elaborate edged compote with a chain like series of loops intersected by diamond shaped elements ending in balls. It is 3 inches tall by 8 inches across and is blue.

Cut Star Compote—A blue piece with two rows of finely cut stars around the bowl and a scalloped edge. It is 3 by 7½ inches.

Ball And Chain Edge Compote   Cut Star Compote

PLATE 87

Doric Border Nappie   Square Cake Salver

PLATE 88

Thumbprint Sauces And Compote

PLATE 89

Doric Border Nappie—An Atterbury creation which shows a simple border with loops. It was made during the 80's and is 11 inches across the top.

Square Cake Salver—A footed and low cake salver with a square body and a fringed edge. It is 6 by 11 inches in size and was made during the 80's.

Thumbprint Sauces And Compote—A rare treat to find these magnificent pieces in a set. It is a Bekewell, Pears & Co., set created during the early 60's.

Grape Tureen—A large tureen with grapes and leaves covering the body of the bowl. It has three scroll-l'ke feet and horn-like processes on the edge. It is a rare piece and hard to find.

Swan Compote—A footed compote of this pattern which shows swans facing on the sides. It is 8 inches across the top.

Grape Tureen   Swan Compote

PLATE 90

Leaf Edge Nappie   Sunflower Boat Nappie

PLATE 91

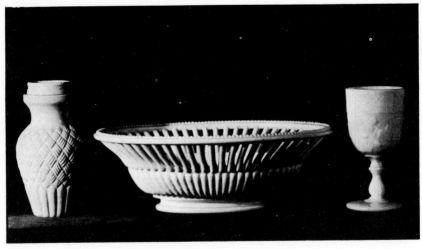

Ribbed Diamond Covered Jar   Beaded Rib, Open Slatted Compote   Ivy In Snow Goblet

PLATE 92

Leaf Edge Nappie—A scalloped edge nappie showing leaves overlapping on the bowl. It is 5½ inches in diameter. It comes in white and blue.

Sunflower Boat Nappie—A boat shaped nappie with sunflowers on the bowl, among scrolls. It is footed and this piece is blue. It is 5 inches wide by 11 inches long.

Ribbed Diamond Covered Jar—A tall tapering jar with tibbed diamonds on the centre of the body. It has flutes below. It is blue.

Beaded Rib, Open Slatted, Compote—A rather large compote without stem and showing open slatted top. It is an Atterbury & Co.'s piece of the 80's.

Ivy In Snow Goblet—A white goblet of this well known pattern, which has a very faintly impressed design on the bowl. It is fairly modern.

White Turtle—A large turtle in plain white which is thought to be modern and of British manufacture.

Entwined Fish, Lacy Edge Dish—A moderate sized dish or compote with fish entwined around the finial of shell type. It is an Atterbury & Co.'s production of the 80's.

White Turtle   Entwined Fish, Lacy Edge Dish

PLATE 93

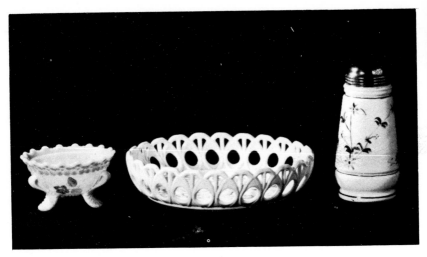

Notched Top
Footed Sauce

Scroll And Eye
Fruit Dish

Flowered Sugar
Shaker

PLATE 94

Beaded Medallion Footed Nappie

Single Loop Edge Nappie

PLATE 95

Notched Top, Footed Sauce—A sauce with looped feet on the sides and a notched edge. It is 3 inches across.

Scroll And Eye Fruit Dish—A rather low type of dish in this Atterbury & Co. pattern. It measures 10 inches across the top.

Flowered Sugar Shaker—A slender type of sugar shaker with a creased body and painted on the surface.

Beaded Medallion, Footed Nappie —A very slender and tall nappie with scalloped top edge and four heavy feet. It is 7 inches tall and 6 inches wide.

Single Loop Edge Nappie—A low type of nappie with a single row of loops around the edge. It is 8½ inches across the top.

Handled Nappie—A crimp edge nappie with handles and a beaded edge. It is a 7 inch piece.

Creased Nappie—A mate to the latter one except the handles and the edges are crimped deeper so that there are deep creases in the sides. It is 7 inches across.

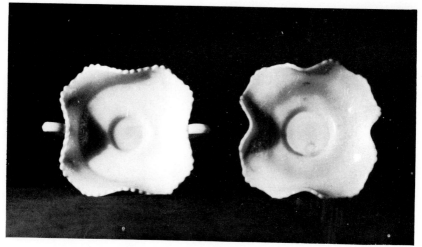

Handled Nappie   Creased Nappie

PLATE 96

Scroll Master Salt   Draped Beaded Dish   Sandwich Boat Salt

PLATE 97

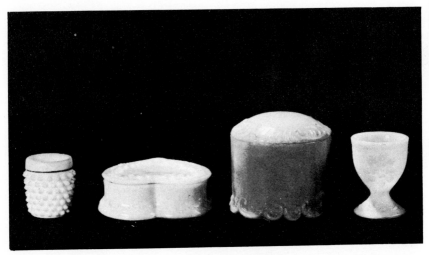

Hobnail
Match

Heart Shaped
Covered Hair Dish

Scroll Foot
Hair Dish

Strawberry
Egg Cup

PLATE 98

Scroll Master Salt—A master salt of this well known pattern.

Draped Beaded Dish—A blue dish 4¾ inches in diameter with draped beads around the bowl.

Sandwich Boat Salt—This sandwich piece is the well known LaFayette Boat and is in blue.

Hobnail Match—A small, modern match box in hobnail with a dark band at the top.

Heart Shaped, Coverd Hair Dish—This is an attractive dresser covered dish in the shape of a heart.

Scroll Foot Hair Dish—A dish with scroll feet and spread over the cover in the same form of primary elements.

Strawberry Egg Cup—The ordinary egg cup with the strawberry design on the sides, which is in this instance rather faintly indented.

Wreath Hair Dish—A covered dish with scroll wreaths around the bowl and a creased foot. A hole in the top.

Rose Lid Trinket Box—A covered dish with roses on the lid. A draped bar wreath around the bottom and scalloped feet.

Open Top Hair Box—A square, covered box with hole in the top. It rests on four feet.

Needle Point Hair Box—A covered dish with needle point like elements on the bowl.

| Wreath Hair Dish | Rose Lid Trinket Box | Open Top Hair Box | Needle Point Hair Box |

PLATE 99

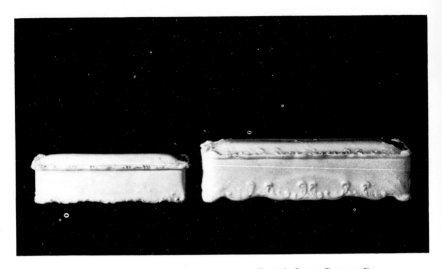

Oblong. Dot and Bar Dresser Box   Footed, Long, Dresser Box

PLATE 100

Milady's Hair Box   Scoop Master Salt   Hexagon Hair Box

PLATE 101

Oblong Dot And Bar Dresser Box—A covered dish with dots and bars on the edge of the lid. It is 2¼ by 7¾ inches.

Footed Long Dresser Box—A covered dish with four feet which measures 3½ by 10 inches in diameter.

Milady's Hair Box—A square box with lid, and scalloped feet.

Scoop Master Salt—A scoop-like salt with handle and standing on four feet.

Hexagon Hair Box—As the name indicates, a covered box which is covered with scrolls painted.

Fedora Hat—A rather large sized hat of the Fedora type.

Fluted Dresser Box—A long covered dish with fluted figure all over. It is 2¾ by 6½ inches. It is blue in color.

Flying Fish Salt—A footed flying fish measuring 4¾ inches long.

Fedora Hat   Fluted Dresser Box   Flying Fish Salt

PLATE 102

Crimped Edge
Bowl

Leaf Footed
Bowl

Iris Deep
Hair Box

PLATE 103

Iris Covered
Jar

Panelled
Scroll Vase

Rose Vase,
Small

Mother And
Child Vase

PLATE 104

Crimped Edge Bowl—A cream colored bowl with four feet and a crimped edge.

Leaf Footed Bowl—A large, round bowl with heavy leaves near the bottom forming feet.

Iris Deep Hair Box—A straight sided and rather tall box with iris on the sides.

Iris Covered Jar—A covered jar with iris on the sides.

Panelled Scroll Vase—A medium sized vase with panelled scrolls on the sides.

Small Rose Vase—A small example of this well known pattern.

Mother And Child Vase—A mother leading child on the sides of this vase which narrows at the top end and is footed.

Ring Footed Egg Cup—A plain egg cup, with tall foot.

Lily Syrup—A bulb type of syrup with lillies on the bowl.

Marble Glass Tumbler—A small tumbler of the purple marble type.

Ring Footed
Plain Egg Cup

Lily Syrup

Marble Glass
Tumbler

PLATE 105

Flowered Vase   Panelled Daisy Covered Jar

PLATE 106

Leaf And Scroll Vase   Scalloped Top Vase   Panelled Grape Vase

PLATE 107

Flowered Vase—A tall vase with a narrow neck and with painted flowers on the bowl. It is 10 inches tall.

Panelled Daisy Covered Jar—A medium sized jar with metal lid and with small daisies on the bowl.

Leaf And Scroll Vase—An attractive vase with raised leaves and scrolls on the body. It is 9 inches tall.

Scalloped Top Vase—A tall vase with narrow neck and a lily-like scalloped top. It is 11 inches tall.

Panelled Grape Vase — A bulb shaped vase with a narrow neck and panelled grapes on the bowl. It is 9 inches tall.

Pyramid Vase—A pyramidal shaped vase with round foot, and scalloped top. It is 8 inches tall.

Hand Vase—An attractive vase in blue with a hand holding a scalloped top cornucopia. It is 8 inches tall.

Straight Sided Plain Vase—A tall, plain white vase which is slightly tapered. It is 8 inches tall.

Pyramid Vase   Hand Vase   Straight Sided, Plain Vase

PLATE 108

Tall Bay Rum Bottle   Ring Handled Platter   Bulb Bottom Vase

PLATE 109

Panelled Flower   Rose Overlay   Panelled Flower
Vase   Vase   Vase

PLATE 110

Tall Bay Rum Bottle—As indicated, a tall bottle with the name in bold letters and painted flowers.

Ring Handled Platter—A long platter with ring handles in each end and scrolls around a scalloped edge. It measures 6 by 8½ inches.

Bulb Bottom Vase—An 8 inch vase with a bulb at the bottom, and a rim top.

Panelled Flower Vases—A pair, one on either side, with flowers raised on the sides and rather ribbed. They are 5¼ inches tall.

Rose Overlay Vase—A tall vase with crimped top and a large rose in colors attached to the bowl. It is 11 inches tall.

Crimped Top Vase—A bulb shaped vase with narrow neck and crimped top. It is 8 inches tall.

Pointed Top Vase—A plain vase with a large bulb bottom and pointed top. It is 10 inches tall.

Daisy Vase—A narrow necked vase with bulb bowl, and with daisies painted on the surface. It is 8 inches tall.

Fluted Vase—A small, narrow vase with fluted sides and large foot. It is 6½ inches tall.

Crimped Top   Pointed Top   Daisy Vase   Fluted Vase
Vase   Vase

PLATE 111

Dog Head Flask	Square Foot Candle Holder	Flower Sugar Shaker	Pyramid Sundae, Pink

PLATE 112

Apple Blossom Jar	Beaded Band Cruet	Swirl Covered Jar

PLATE 113

Dog Head Flask—A fairly large flask with a dog head on the side. It is of French origin.

Square Foot Candle Holder—A medium tall candle holder with a square foot and a wide lip at the top.

Flower Sugar Shaker—A small sized sugar shaker with flowers painted on the bowl. It is creased below and above.

Pyramid Sundae Pink—A pyramidal shaped sundae which is of pink marble glass and is of the fluted pattern. It is rare in this color.

Apple Blossom Jar—An open jar of the flare top type, showing apple blossoms painted on the sides.

Beaded Band Cruet—A vinegar cruet of pink marble glass and hard to find. Evidently a trial piece for they are not found often.

Swirl Covered Jar—A jar with a definite swirl type of element. It comes in white and blue.

Oval Plain Covered Jar—A bulge type of covered jar in the plain white.

Rose Covered Jar—A large, footed, covered jar with a rose as a finial for the top and a large rose on the sides. It is footed and comes in white and blue.

Owl Covered Jar—A tall jar with owl head and body for the jar. It comes in white and blue.

Oval, Plain Covered Jar   Rose Covered Jar   Owl Covered Jar

PLATE 114

Hand Compote   Fluted Compote

PLATE 115

Lattice Compote   Scroll Compote

PLATE 116

Hand Compote—A large, round bowl measuring 7¼ inches across and a hand stem on a ribbed base. It is 8 inches tall.

Fluted Compote—A fluted bowl with what some have called a Jenny Lind bust for the stem. It is 7 inches tall and measures 7 inches across the top.

Lattice Compote—An Atterbury product with daisy and button stem and foot. It measures 7¼ inches across the bowl and is 7½ inches tall.

Scroll Compote—A deep bowl compote of the scroll type with a bulb stem. It is 7¼ inches across the top and is 7¼ inches tall.

Low Lattice Compote— Here is a shallow, latticed bowl with basket weave stem and foot. It is 8 inches across the top and 6¼ inches tall. Atterbury & Co.

Lattice Edged Cake Stand— A large cake stand measuring 8½ inches across the top and with fluted stem and foot. It is 7¼ inches tall.

Low Lattice Compote   Lattice Edge Cake Stand

PLATE 117

Blackberry Sugar   PLATE 118   Blackberry Compote

Ribbed Compote   Tree of Life Compote

PLATE 119

Blackberry Sugar—A covered sugar with a large berry as knob to top and on sides as handles. It is of the early 70's.

Blackberry Compote—A covered compote in this well known pattern measuring 12 inches tall. It also is of the same period.

Ribbed Compote—A tall, covered compote with ribbed bowl and lid. It has a tripod stem and is 13 inches tall.

Tree Of Life Compote—A Portland Glass Co. product with cover. It comes in plain and painted surface.

Melon Compote—Here is a footed compote of this well known type which is 6½ inches long.

Robin On Nest Compote—A product of Indiana Goblet and Tumbler Co., of Greentown, Ind., and measures 6¼ inches in diameter. It rests on four feet and has a round base covered with flowers. Made at Greentown, Indiana.

Melon Compote   Robin On Nest Compote

PLATE 120

Basket Weave Compote   Deep Lattice Compote

PLATE 121

Panelled Flower Compote   Ribbed Stem Compote

PLATE 122

Basket Weave Compote—A large piece with a basket weave design on the body. It has a deep bowl and measures 8 inches tall and 7 inches across the top.

Deep Lattice Compote—A rather deep bowl of this Atterbury & Co. piece, with a basket weave stem. It is 7 inches tall and 7½ inches in diameter.

Panelled Flower .Compote — A medium sized compote with bold flower paintings on the sides and scalloped top. It is 6¾ inches tall and 7½ inches wide at the top.

Ribbed Stem Compote—A tall compote with ribbed stem and a single row of loops around the top edge. It is 9 inches tall by 7 inches wide.

Flared Lattice Compote—The usual lacy edge compote but rather deep in the bowl. It is an Atterbury & Co. product of the 80's. It is 7 inches tall and 8¾ inches wide.

Hercules Stem Compote—Here is a tall, lacy edge compote with a man holding the body. It has been called a number of names but this one seems appropriate. It is 8½ inches tall and 8¼ inches wide. It is an Atterbury product.

Flared Lattice Compote   Hercules Stem Compote

PLATE 123

Hobnail Compote   Tall Melon Compote

PLATE 124

Plain. Ringed Foot Cake Stand   Fluted Cake Stand

PLATE 125

Hobnail Compote—A tall compote of this pattern which is fairly modern. It is a desirable piece at best. It is 7½ inches tall and 9 inches across the top.

Tall Melon Compote—Another of the melon type of compote with a metal connector between the foot and the bowl. It is 12 inches tall and 8 inches in diameter.

Plain Ringed Foot Cake Stand— A tall cake stand with ringed foot and stem. They are usually painted. It is 6¼ inches tall and 9 inches across.

Fluted Cake Stand—An example of the fluted pattern which is 6 inches tall and 10 inches across the top. It was made by Atterbury & Co.

Square Leaf Syrup—A square syrup with oak leaves on the sides and an applied handle.

Corn Sugar Shaker — A sugar shaker in the form of an ear of corn, with shucks below on the bowl.

Beaded Panel Syrup—A beaded panel separates flower-like scrolls on the body. It has an applied handle.

Square Leaf Syrup   Corn Sugar Shaker   Beaded Panel Syrup

PLATE 126

Hexagon Syrup   Poppy Syrup   Scalloped Rib Syrup

PLATE 127

Pyramid Syrup   Beaded Scroll Syrup   Ribbed Sugar Shaker

PLATE 128

Hexagon Syrup—A plain hexagon shaped syrup.

Poppy Syrup—A bulb shaped bowl showing poppies painted on the bowl. It has an applied handle.

Scalloped Rib Syrup—A bulb shaped bowl with scalloped ribs above and below, with applied handle.

Pyramid Syrup—A painted, pyramid shaped syrup with applied handle.

Beaded Scroll Syrup—A painted panel syrup with panels marked by rows of beads. An applied handle.

Ribbed Sugar Shaker—A small sugar shaker with ribs all over the surface and a metal cap.

Panelled Scroll Syrup—Here is an attractive syrup of a panelled scroll type with applied handle.

Handled Candle Holder—A low type of holder in blue, with a ringed handle.

Plain White Vase—A vase of plain white with a bulb base and ringed top.

Panelled Scroll Syrup   Handled Candle Holder   Plain White Vase

PLATE 129

Heavy Scroll Syrup   Bell Flower Syrup   Leaf Syrup

PLATE 130

Strawberry Syrup   Fern And Scroll Syrup   Stippled Dahlia Syrup

PLATE 131

Heavy Scroll Syrup—A syrup with heavy type of scroll at top and bottom, and applied handle.

Bell Flower Syrup—A rare piece of this well known pattern with an applied handle. Made in the 60's.

Leaf Syrup—A slender body syrup showing leaves on surface.

Strawberry Syrup—A large syrup with heavy design of strawberries on the bowl and a tall piece.

Fern And Scroll Syrup—A neat type of syrup with ferns, ribs and scrolls on the surface. It has an applied handle.

Stippled Dahlia Syrup—A syrup showing the upper part of the bowl covered by fine stippling and dahlias in panels.

Large Swan Salt—An attractive salt in the shape of a large swan with wings forming sides. A Sandwich piece.

Beaded Rib Tumbler—A tumbler with panelled sides formed by rows of beads. Rather tall tumbler.

Swirl Syrup—A small syrup with swirl body and applied handle.

Large Swan Salt   Beaded Rib Tumbler   Swirl Syrup

PLATE 132

Grape Handled Sugar   Jacob's Coat Butter   Pineapple Creamer

PLATE 133

Bee Hive Sugar   Ribbed, Lacy Edge Covered Sugar   Ibsen Sugar

PLATE 134

Grape Handled Sugar—A covered sugar in this well known pattern. With handles and a knob finial. It is rather scarce. Made during the 70's.

Jacob's Coat Butter—A butter probably made from the original molds which were used during the 80's to make crystal glass pieces in the pattern. It is rather scarce.

Pineapple Creamer—A desirable piece showing the pattern outstanding on the sides of the piece. It is an early pattern.

Bee Hive Sugar—This is a gypsum piece with cover. It is on the shape of a bee-hive. It must have been a trial piece.

Ribbed. Lacy Edge, Covered Sugar—A pretty covered sugar with flowers painted on the bowl. It is an Atterbury piece of the 80's.

Ibsen Sugar— A trial piece that is well known to dealers and collectors. It is rather scarce. It shows various figures on the panels.

Tulip Butter—A rare piece made by Bryce Brothers in the 60's and hard to find.

Arch Edged Fruit Dish—A flat like dish with arched edge open to the bottom. It is an 8 inch dish.

Bird Shaped Pickle — A small pickle in the shape of a bird. It is pink in color.

Tulip Butter   Arch Edged Fruit Dish   Bird Shaped Pickle
PLATE 135

Grant's Tomb
Bottle

Long Neck
Bottle

Bulb Neck
Bottle

Ring Handle
Bottle

PLATE 136

Pipe And Bowl Flask

Apple Blossom Vase

PLATE 137

Grant's Tomb Bottle—A short bottle representing General Grant's tomb. It is rare.

Long Neck Bottle—A very tall bottle with a long neck. Pint size.

Bulb Neck Bottle—Another fairly tall bottle with bulb bowl and also a bulb on the neck, making it rather odd in shape.

Ring Handle Bottle—A tall bottle with an applied ring handle near the top.

Pipe And Bowl Flask—A large flask in the shape of a happy man's body. He holds a pipe in one hand and a glass in the other. It is a very desirable piece.

Apple Blossom Vase—A tall vase, straight sided except near the bottom, where it bulges, and with apple blossoms painted on the body.

Ruffled Top Rose Overlay Vase— A short vase with large rose and leaves in overlay on the sides. It is rare.

Sacred Crucifix Candle Holder— A tall candle holder formed by a cross held by a priest.

Wreath Scroll Covered Bottle—A bulb body bottle with fine scrolls on the bowl and a large stopper.

Ruffled Top Rose
Overlay Vase

Sacred Crucifix
Candle Holder

Wreath Scroll
Covered Bottle

PLATE 138

Fluted Flask   Bay Rum Bottle   Cologne Bottle

PLATE 139

Wich Hazel Bottle   Bulb Bottom Bottle

PLATE 140

Fluted Flask—A large flask with flutes covering the body.

Bay Rum Bottle—A slender, tall bottle with label painted on surface.

Cologne Bottle—A squarish type of bottle with a narrow foot. 8 inches tall. It is a French product.

Wich Hazel Bottle—A tall, tapering bottle with stippled neck and a fluted base. A plain space for label. 9¼ inches tall.

Bulb Bottom Bottle—A tall dresser bottle with round stopper which is large. 11 inches tall.

Scroll Footed Bottle—A nice bottle resting on four scroll feet, and with crown top stopper. 9 inches tall.

Beaded Circle Milk Pitcher—A blue milk pitcher with well marked beaded circles near the foot. It is 9 inches tall.

Actress Head Bottle—An elaborate bottle, highly decorated and showing an actress head in medallions. It is 10 inches tall.

Scroll Footed Bottle   Beaded Circle Milk Pitcher   Actress Head Bottle

PLATE 141

Plain Oval Tray   French Cologne Bottle

PLATE 142

Draped Scroll Bottle   Gargoyle Head Bottle

PLATE 143

Plain Oval Dresser Tray—A large shallow tray measuring 8½ inches across the top.

French Cologne Bottle—A rather tall bottle with French inscription on the sides. It is 7½ inches tall.

Draped Scroll Bottle—A rather tall bottle with draped scrolls on the body. It is 9½ inches tall.

Gargoyle Head Bottle—A large bulbed bowl bottle with gargoyle heads near the base. It is 9 inches tall.

Scroll Bottom Bottle—A bottle with a large bulb bowl and slender neck. It is 8 inches tall.

Wide Lipped Bottle—A large bulbed bottle and slender neck with a wide lip around the top. It is 9 inches tall.

Scroll Bottom Bottle   Wide Lipped Bottle

PLATE 144

Leaf Bottle   Iris Water Pitcher

PLATE 145

Cosmos Water Pitcher   Ferns And Birds Water Pitcher

PLATE 146

Leaf Bottle—A bulb shaped dresser bottle with leaves extending upward from the foot. It is 7½ inches tall.

Iris Water Pitcher—An elaborate water pitcher, bulb shaped, and a crimped top, with Iris painted on the sides. It is 9 inches tall.

Cosmos Water Pitcher—A large sized pitcher with a diamond lacing over the bowl and cosmos tinted flowers superimposed. It is 8 inches tall.

Ferns And Birds Water Pitcher—A tall pitcher with ribbed base below and flying birds among crossed ferns on the bowl. It is 9 inches in height.

Cherry Overlay Pitcher—A very attractive pitcher with an elaborate body and top. It has colored cherries and leaves overlaying the sides. It is 8 inches tall.

Satin Overlay Pitcher—Here is a truly overlay pitcher with a delicate satin feel. It has a crimped top and applied handle. It is 7 inches tall.

Cherry Overlay Pitcher   Satin Overlay Pitcher

PLATE 147

Ivy Covered Jar   Covered Urn   Square Scroll Covered Jar

PLATE 148

Yellow Marble   Sawtooth Covered   Hobnail   Corn
Match   Bottle   Tumbler   Vase

PLATE 149

Ivy Covered Jar—A rather low bulbed shape jar with lid and covered with ivy and vines.

Covered Urn—An elaborate urn with handles and ribbed cover, and crossed flower stems on the bowl. It is 8 inches tall.

Square Scroll Covered Jar—A square, low typed jar with cover and showing scroll-like elements over the corners of the bowl.

Yellow Marble Match—The familiar type of tall match holder in yellow marble glass.

Sawtooth Covered Bottle—A large mouthed bottle with sawtooth on the lower part of the bowl and stopper.

Hobnail Tumbler—An ordinary sized tumbler with four rows of hobs and a dark beaded band. It is a modern piece.

Corn Vase—An attractive vase showing an ear of corn with shucks on the body.

Cosmos Milk Pitcher—A two quart pitcher of the same type as a former cut of the water pitcher.

Emerging Chicks on Basket—A handled basket with chicks emerging from numerous eggs.

Open Urn, Blue—A similar piece to the covered urn shown but this one has no lid and is in blue.

Cosmos Milk Pitcher   Emerging Chicks On Basket   Open Urn, Blue

PLATE 150

Knotted Cord Creamer   Princess Feather Spooner   Panelled Shell Creamer

PLATE 151

Scalloped Top
Covered Creamer   Footed Dahlia
Covered Creamer   Panelled Shell
Milk Pitcher

PLATE 152

Knotted Cord Creamer—A very attractive creamer of green color and showing cord diamonds in knotted form of the bowl.

Princess Feather Spooner—An example of this well known pattern in milk white glass.

Panelled Shell Creamer—A very desirable pattern with panelled areas containing shells and a beaded bottom.

Scalloped Top Covered Creamer— A squarish creamer with scalloped top and lid.

Footed Dahlia Covered Creamer— A very pretty creamer with 8 feet and dahlias on the corners.

Panelled Shell Milk Pitcher—A mate to the creamer above but with slightly differing shape.

Block And Fan Creamer—An open creamer of this well known pattern and very attractive.

Wheat Creamer—A tall creamer of the panelled wheat pattern and very rare. Made by Hobbs, Brockunier & Co., of Wheeling, W. Va., during the 70's.

Beaded Jewel Creamer—A very pretty creamer with fine beads around the bowl and on the handle.

Block And Fan Creamer   Wheat Creamer   Beaded Jewel Creamer

PLATE 153

Ribbed Shell Creamer   Swan Creamer   Raised Grape Creamer

PLATE 154

Blackberry Spooner   Wheat Milk Pitcher   Grape Spooner

PLATE 155

Ribbed Shell Creamer—A very bold type of creamer with a plain belt between ribbed shells above and below. An applied handle.

Swan Creamer—As the name would indicate there are swans on the bowl, and a large spout.

Raised Grape Creamer—A pattern showing grapes and leaves raised above the surface in a bold manner. An applied handle is shown.

Blackberry Spooner — Another piece of this well known pattern and hard to find at best.

Wheat Milk Pitcher—A small milk pitcher of the panelled wheat pattern, in two quart size. A product of Hobbs, Brockuneir & Co., of Wheeling, W. Va., in the 70's.

Grape Spooner—An example of the usual grape pattern and a very desirable piece.

Creased Scroll Syrup—A syrup with deep creases in the body of the bowl and with an applied handle.

Stippled Dahlia Syrup, Blue—Here is a duplicate of a former one shown but is in blue color and no top.

Diamond Point Syrup—A painted type of syrup and with diamond points below. It has an applied handle.

Creased Scroll Syrup   Stippled Dahlia Syrup, Blue   Diamond Point Syrup

PLATE 156

Chick Salt   Footed Salt   Fruit Wine   Chick Salt

PLATE 157

Panelled   Mustard   Tall Scroll   Knobby
Scroll Salt   Bulb   Salt   Salt

PLATE 158

Chick Salts—A pair of chick salts with metal heads, on either end of this cut.

Footed Salt—A lobular bulbed salt with beaded foot.

Fruit Wine—A small wine of the fruit type, measuring 3¾ inches tall. Modern.

Panelled Scroll Salt—A rather tall salt with panelled scrolls on the bowl.

Bulb Mustard—A bulb shaped body mustard jar with flowers painted on the bowl.

Tall Scroll Salt—A narrow neck salt with heavy scrolls on the bowl and footed.

Knobby Salt — A salt showing heavy scrolls above and below on the body, with a constricted centre.

Beaded Belt Match—A low type of match holder with a beaded belt which narrows the centre.

Panelled Rib Salt—A footed salt with deep flutes and beads on the ribs.

Tulip Salt — An attractive salt showing tulip petals on the sides.

Egg Salt—A salt in the shape of an egg with metal cap.

Beaded Belt Match   Panelled Rib Salt   Tulip Salt   Egg Salt

PLATE 159

Bulge Bottom
Salt
 Lobulated
Pepper
 Beaded Bottom
Salt
 Ribbed
Salt

PLATE 160

Dahlia Salt Lobulated Salt Daisy Salt Panelled Flower Salt

PLATE 161

Bulge Bottom Salt—As the name indicates here is a salt with a wide, sharp bulge in the base.

Lobulated Pepper—A pepper with lobulated sides and beaded base.

Beaded Bottom Salt—A wide base salt with beaded bottom.

Ribbed Salt—A salt showing a ribbed section on the lower part of the bowl.

Dahlia Salt—A salt with bold dahlias outstanding on the bowl.

Lobulated Salt—A mate to the pepper shown above.

Daisy Salt—A large salt with daisies painted on the surface.

Panelled Flower Salt—A salt with panells separating raised flowers on the bowl.

Lobulated Mustard—A mate to the salt and pepper shown above.

Creased Scroll Salt—A salt showing deep creases in the bowl and raised scrolls on the bowl.

Square Scroll Salt—A tall salt with square outline and heavy scrolls on the body.

Panelled Shell Salt—A heavy rough type of salt with shell figures overlapping on the bowl.

Lobulated   Creased Scroll   Square Scroll   Panelled Shell
Mustard   Salt   Salt   Salt

PLATE 162

Grape Salt   Beaded Panel   Rib Footed   Flute Salt
Salt   Salt

PLATE 163

Beaded Top   Triple Swan   Owl Match   Goose Salt
Kettle   Match

PLATE 164

Grape Salt—A salt with large grapes on the body.

Beaded Panel Salt—A salt with beaded panels and painted.

Rib Footed Salt—Here is a salt with heavy ribbed feet.

Flute Salt—A fluted salt with wide foot.

Beaded Top Kettle—A white kettle with a beaded top.

Triple Swan Match—A holder with three swan necks and heads.

Owl Match—A match holder with out stretched wings of an owl.

Goose Salt—A master salt in the form of a goose.

Cactus Salt—A tall salt with cactus like forms above and below.

Pineapple Salt—A salt with pineapple figure on the body.

Swirl Salt—A tall salt with constricted centre and swirls at the top and bottom.

Draped Leaf Salt—A squatty salt with overlapping leaves on the body.

Cactus Salt   Pineapple Salt   Swirl Salt   Draped Leaf Salt

PLATE 165

| Apple Blossom | Footed Scroll | Creased | Plain Sugar |
| Salt | Salt | Salt | Shaker |

PLATE 166

| Double | Creased | Peach | Corn | Hexagon |
| Rib Salt | Neck Salt | Blossom Salt | Salt | Pyramid Salt |

PLATE 167

Apple Blossom Salt—A straight sided salt with crease near the top and apple blossoms painted on the bowl.

Footed Scroll Salt—A salt shaker with square outline and large scrolls on the corners.

Creased Salt—A bulb bottom salt with a deep crease dividing the bowl.

Plain Sugar Shaker—A slender, tall, sugar shaker with plain sides.

Double Rib Salt—A tall salt with ribs below and above on the bowl.

Creased Neck Salt—A medium salt with a crease around the neck and painted.

Peach Blossom Salt—A creased neck salt with peach blossoms painted on the body.

Corn Salt—A small salt representing an ear of corn.

Hexagon Pyramid Salt—A pyramidal shaped salt with hexagon sides and scroll feet.

Panelled Daisy Salt—A beaded panel encloses daisies.

Knotty Bulb Salt—Here is a salt with a knotty like body and narrow neck.

Guttate Salt—Socalled from its fancy resemblance to drops of heavy liquid.

Twisted Scroll Salt—A scroll salt of more than usual height, with a twisted scroll on the body. It is blue in color.

Diamond Block Salt—Here the blocks are diamond shaped on a squatty type of holder.

| Panelled Daisy Salt | Knotty Bulb Salt | Guttate Salt | Twisted Scroll Salt, Blue | Diamond Block Salt |

PLATE 168

| Spider-web
Salt | Orange
Covered Dish | Anvil
Salt | Horse-shoe &
Clover Salt |

PLATE 169

| Lemon Salt | Circular Ink Well | Chicken Salt |

PLATE 170

Spider-webb Salt—A squatty salt with spider-webb design.

Orange Covered Dish—A small dish with cover, showing orange leaves, and the body shaped like an orange.

Anvil Salt—A daisy and button salt of an anvil shape.

Horse-shoe And Clover Salt—A square salt with horse-shoe on the sides and a clover leaf within the shoe.

Lemon Salt—A small salt in the shape of a lemon and of the color of lemon.

Circular Ink Well—A medium ink well in circular form and with a large pear on top.

Chicken Salt—A salt in the shape of a chicken body.

Low Scroll Salt—A low salt with heavy, parted, scrolls on the body.

Rabbit Salt—A bulbed salt with a rabbit on each side.

Horse-shoe salt—A square salt with horse-shoe on the sides.

Hen Salt— A bulbed shape salt with a hen on the sides.

Cotton Bale Salt—A salt which resembles a cotton bale.

Low Scroll   Rabbit   Horse Shoe   Hen   Cotton Bale
Salt   Salt   Match   Salt   Salt

PLATE 171

| Basket Weave | Swirl Sugar | World's Fair | Scroll Footed |
| Salt | Shaker | Candle Holder | Salt |

PLATE 172

| Palm and Bull's | Pyramid Candle | Ivy Cruet | Panelled Footed |
| Eye Candle | Holder | | Salt |

PLATE 173

Basket Weave Salt—A low salt in the basket weave type.

Swirl Sugar Shaker—A tall, slender sugar shaker with swirls on the base of the body.

World's Fair Candle Holder—A tall, pyramidal holder with fine scrolls on the body.

Scroll Footed Salt—A low individual salt with scroll feet.

Palm And Bull's Eye Candle Holder—An attractive low type of holder as indicated.

Pyramid Candle Holder—A tall, pyramid shaped candle holder with scroll feet.

Ivy Cruet—A small white cruet covered with fine ivy.

Panelled Footed Salt—A small salt with ribbed body, cut into panels by dark lines.

Scroll Sauce—A low sauce in this well known pattern.

Printed Hobnail Set—A small condiment set on tray in this well known pattern. It is modern.

Strawberry Sauce—A very low sauce in the strawberry pattern.

Scroll Sauce   Printed Hobnail Set   Strawberry Sauce

PLATE 174

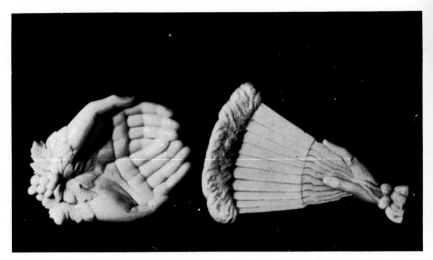

Double Hands With Grapes   Hand And Fan

PLATE 175

Sandwich Dolphin Candle Sticks

PLATE 176

Double Hands With Grapes—A card tray or nappie in the shape of hands together and grapes at the wrist. They were produced by Atterbury & Co., and measure 5¾ by 7½ inches.

Hand And Fan—Another ornamental piece showing a hand holding a fan partially open. It is also an Atterbury product. It is 9 inches long.

Sandwich Dolphin Candle Sticks—Little need be said about these well known rarities. They are very opalescent as the cut would indicate. They belong in the splendid private collection of Mrs. Alexander Janssen of Kansas City, Mo., and are very rare.

Crucifix Candle Sticks—A pair of very attractive candle sticks with crucifix affixed. They have a hexagon base and are rare.

Crucifix Candle Sticks

PLATE 177

Panelled Shell
Cup and Saucer

Panelled Rib
Match Holder

Rose Cup And
Saucer

PLATE 178

Sugar Scoop

Klondyke Flask

Covered Couch Dish

PLATE 179

Panelled Shell Cup And Saucer— A cup and saucer showing beaded bands and panelled shell design. Cups and saucers are not common in white glass.

Panelled Rib Match Holder— A large match holder with four panelled ribs on the sides.

Rose Cup And Saucer— A neat cup and saucer with raised roses, in impressive manner, on the cup and sides of the saucer. It is fairly modern but desirable.

Sugar Scoop— A scoop for sugar with fine scrolls on the surface.

Klondyke Flask— A flask made during the gold rush in the klondyke. It was painted in gilt paint.

Covered Couch Dish— Here is a small couch like dish with a cover and gaudily painted. It is not very common.

Split Rib Mug— A mug showing the split or disjointed ribs.

Sunflower Tumbler— A large flaring top tumbler, with foot. It panels the sunflowers on all sides.

Dart Bar Tumbler— A very white tumbler with dart bars in the centre of the body.

Split Rib Mug   Sunflower Tumbler   Dart Bar Tumbler

PLATE 180

Sailor Hat   Butterfly   Daisy And Button
        Match Holder   Plug Hat

PLATE 181

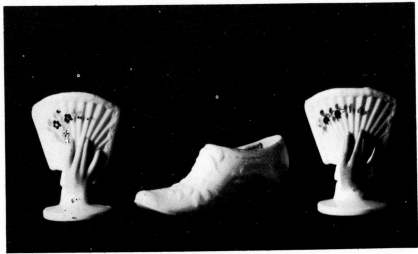

Hand And Fan Match Holder Large Slipper Hand And Fan Match Holder

PLATE 182

Sailor Hat—A hat representing a straw sailor type, with colored band.

Butterfly Match Holder—A match holder in the shape and design of a butterfly.

Daisy And Button Plug Hat—A tall plug hat of this well known pattern.

Hand And Fan Match Holders—A pair of match holders in this design.

Large Slipper—A very white slipper of extreme size. It shows flowers on the surface, otherwise plain.

Handled Basket Sauce—A handled sauce of the basket weave type and very desirable.

Lacy Edge Shell Nappie—A shell shaped nappie with lacy edge and a ribbed centre.

Block Border Sauce—A footed sauce with block border at the top.

Handled Basket Sauce   Lacy Edge Shell Nappie   Block Border Sauce

PLATE 183

Ribbed Swirl
Candle Stick

Ribbed Base Ram

Ribbed Swirl
Candle Stick

PLATE 184

Saucer Candle Holder

Footed Candle Holder

PLATE 185

Ribbed Swirl Candle Sticks—A pair of these attractive, small candle sticks in blue. They are 3½ inches tall.

Ribbed Base Ram—A small covered dish with ribbed base and a horned ram on the cover. It is 3 inches in diameter.

Saucer Candle Holder—A low saucer type of candle holder with a ring handle and is in the blue.

Footed Candle Holder—A low candle holder with 8 feet which are painted. It has a ring handle.

Grape Mug—A small handled mug with small grape design on the sides.

Little "Bo Peep" Platter—A shell shaped platter with the figure of a young lad lying in its folds. It is rare and unusual. The measurements are 6¼ by 8¾ inches.

Draped Bead Cup—A small cup showing draped beads around the bowl. It is opalescent.

Grape Mug   Little "Bo Peep" Platter   Draped Bead Cup

PLATE 186

Owl Creamer   Plain Egg Cup   Grape Sugar Shaker   Cornucopia Match

PLATE 187

Leaf Covered Hair Box   Twisted Scroll Salt   Rose Covered Hair Box

PLATE 188

Owl Creamer—This piece comes in white and blue and usually shows glass eyes.

Plain Egg Cup—A tall egg cup with double ring foot and plain.

Grape Sugar Shaker—A rather small sugar shaker with large grapes on the bowl.

Cornucopia Match—A match holder in cornucopia shape with upper edge painted.

Leaf Covered Hair Box—A covered container for the dresser, with leaves painted on the body.

Twisted Scroll Salt—A tall salt of the swirl scroll type and very attractive.

Rose Covered Hair Box—A piece showing veined leaves for the body and an open rose for the lid.

Ribbed Mug—A tall mug with a section of ribs on the foot and the lower part of the bowl.

Scalloped Salt—A low footed salt with scalloped feet and top.

Panelled Scroll Mug—A large handled mug showing scroll panels.

Ribbed Mug   Scalloped Salt   Panelled Scroll Mug

PLATE 189

Shell Mug   Juniper Salt   Flutted Mug

PLATE 190

Footed Open Box   Cosmos Tumbler   Waffle Tumbler   Grape Tumbler

PLATE 191

Shell Mug—The usual type of shell pattern in a handled mug.

Juniper Salt—A small bulbous type of salt with daisies raised on the surface.

Fluted Mug—A handled mug with bold flutes on the lower part of the body.

Footed Open Box—A dresser container with shell feet and scrolls upward from the feet.

Cosmos Tumbler—A tumbler matching pitchers illustrated elsewhere in the book.

Waffle Tumbler—A very attractive tumbler with well defined waffle elements on the body.

Grape Tumbler—A tumbler with heavy colored grapes on the sides, with vines, and a stippled body.

Blackberry Egg Cup—An egg cup of this well known pattern.

Scroll Tumbler—A tumbler with heavy scrolls on the sides.

Split Rib Tumbler—Another attractive tumbler with broken or split ribs on the sides.

Butterfly Egg Cup—An egg cup with butterflies and flowers painted on the sides.

| Blackberry Egg Cup | Scroll Tumbler | Split Rib Tumbler | Butterfly Egg Cup |

PLATE 192

Tree Of Life   World's Fair   Ribbed Fluted   Monk Stein
Tumbler   Tumbler   Tumbler

PLATE 193

Northwood   Panelled   Acorn Overlay   Basket Weave
Tumbler   Waffle Tumbler   Vase   Egg Cup

PLATE 194

Tree Of Life Tumbler—An attractive tumbler of this well known pattern.

World's Fair Tumbler—A piece made for the World's Fair and very desirous. Of the 90's.

Ribbed Fluted Tumbler—A neat type of tumbler with alternate flutes and ribs.

Monk Stein—A small stein with monks on the sides.

Northwood Tumbler—This piece is shown here because it is a tumbler, but it belongs to the Custard glass section. 4 inches tall.

Panelled Waffle Tumbler—A pretty, footed tumbler with panelled waffle design, well defined. 4½ inches tall.

Acorn Overlay Vase—A very attractive vase of the small type with a dark colored acorn and a large leaf overlaid on the body. 4½ inches tall.

Basket Weave Egg Cup—As the name indicates here is a well defined example of this pattern 3¾ inches tall.

Bar And Swirl Mug—A nice mug with bar and swirl alternating in a band near the foot.

Block And Oval Sauce—A footed sauce with the design well delineated on the body.

Swan Mug—A handled mug in this well known design.

Bar And Swirl Mug   Block And Oval Sauce   Swan Mug

PLATE 195

Square Footed   Scroll Basket   Beaded Match   Blackberry
Match   Footed Sauce

PLATE 196

Plug Hat   Boat Salt   Good Luck   Creased
Match   Bale Salt

PLATE 197

Square Footed Match—A match holder with shell feet and square in outline.

Scroll Basket—A blue colored basket with scroll elements on the sides. Provided with wire handle.

Beaded Match—A flare bottom match holder with three rows of beads around the body.

Blackberry Footed Sauce—A desirable piece of this well known pattern.

Plug Hat—A small plug shaped hat with circular rings around the body and rim.

Boat Salt—A master salt in the shape of a painted boat.

Good Luck Match—Here is a match holder showing a horse-shoe around the holder.

Creased Bale Salt—An attractive salt of expanded bulb body and three constrictions in the body.

Scalloped Edge Boat Salt—A boat salt, in blue, with the edges scalloped.

Chick Head Salt—A large master salt in the shape of an egg with a painted chick head.

Uncle Sam Hat—A campaigne hat in red, white and blue colors, used in campaigns.

Scalloped Edge Boat Salt   Chick Head Salt   Uncle Sam Hat

PLATE 198

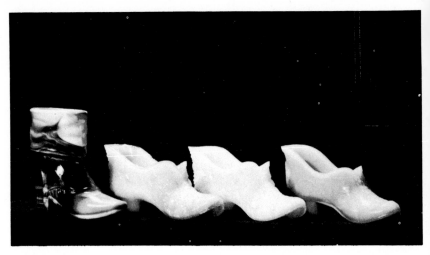

Marble Glass
Boot

Daisy and Button
Slipper

Checkered
Slipper

Plain
Slipper

PLATE 199

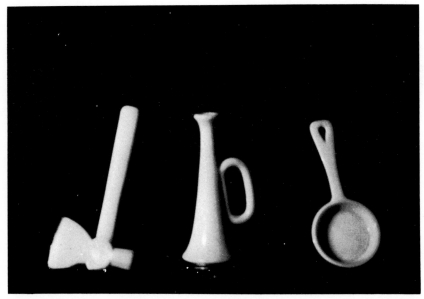

Hatchet

Trumpet

Skillet

PLATE 200

Marble Glass Boot—An attractive example of a purple marble glass piece which is in the shape of a high boot.

Daisy And Button Slipper—An example of a shoe in this well known pattern. Probably modern.

Checkered Slipper—Here is a slipper checkered on the sides and of similar proportions to the daisy and button slipper.

Plain Slipper—A plain white slipper, with scrolls on the sides.

Hatchet—A trinket made in the shape of a hatchet, in plain white.

Trumpet—Another trinket in the shape of a trumpet and in white.

Skillet—A plain white trinket in the shape of an ordinary skillet.

Sandwich Curtain Tie Backs—A pair of these desirable and rare tie backs in white.

Book Match—A match holder in the shape of a book.

Pipe Match—An unusual match holder, using the bowl of a pipe for the holder.

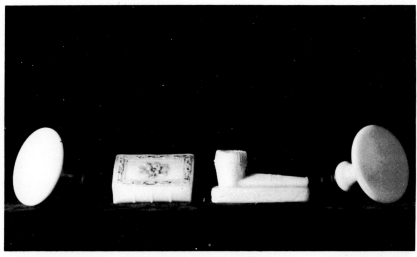

Sandwich   Curtain   Book Match   Pipe Match   Sandwich Curtain
      Tie-backs   Tie-backs

PLATE 201

Little Red Riding Hood Set
PLATE 202

Flute Sauce   Sprinkler   Bead Handled Mug
PLATE 203

Little Red Riding Hood—A junior set of bowl and six sauces in blue, with design of Little Red Riding Hood.

Flute Sauce—A footed sauce in the familar pattern.

Sprinkler—A milk white glass toy in the shape of a small sprinkler.

Bead Handled Mug—A mug with large beads forming the handle and with a ribbed base.

Covered Strawberry Dish—An attractive and rare piece in the shape of a large strawberry, with a snail on the lid.

Condiment Set—A small white condiment set with metal caps and metal carrier.

Herring Bone Butter—A covered butter in this pattern. It is scarce. It was created during the early 80's.

Covered Strawberry Dish   Condiment Set   Herringbone Butter

PLATE 204

Cross Fern Butter   Oblong Sawtooth Covered Dish   Lacy Edged Bowl

PLATE 205

Crown Top Sugar   Lacy Top, Ribbed Creamer And Sugar

PLATE 206

Cross Fern Butter—A covered butter measuring 6¼ inches across, in this well known pattern.

Oblong Sawtooth Covered Dish—A very desirable piece of this pattern which is handled. It comes in two sizes. 3½ by 5¼ inches and 4¼ by 6½ inche dimensions.

Lacy Edged Bowl—A rather low type of bowl with broad lacy edge. It is an Atterbury product. It measures 7 inches across the top.

Crown Top Sugar—A covered sugar with four legs, a fluted base and a crown cover.

Lacy Top, Ribbed Creamer And Sugar—A pair of Atterbury Co. Pieces with lacy tops and ribbed base below a wide plain band.

Panelled Shell Sugar—A covered sugar in the panelled shell pattern.

Twin Horn Sugar—A covered sugar and as indicated a twin horn pattern. It is blue.

Ribbed, Covered Sugar—A covered sugar with ribbed base and cover, and a plain band between.

Panelled Shell Sugar   Twin Horn Sugar   Ribbed Covered Sugar

PLATE 207

Panelled Fern Spooner   Thumbprint Spooner   Plain Tumbler

PLATE 208

Daisy, Crimped   Daisy and Button   Grape, Ruffled
Top Dish   Sauce   Top Nappie

PLATE 209

Panelled Fern Spooner—A very desirable piece in this pattern which has ferns on the raised sections and deep creases between them.

Thumbprint Spooner—A very rare pieces in this pattern. White glass pieces are hard to find in thumbprint.

Plain Tumbler—A tall, plain tumbler in white.

Daisy, Crimped Top Dish—A dish or nappie with ruffled top.

Daisy And Button Sauce—A sauce of low type in this well known pattern.

Grape Ruffled Top Nappie—A very unusual piece in shape and showing large grapes on the surface.

Mosaic Creamer—A blue piece with rich mosaic design on the sides. It is rather scarce.

Basket Weave Tumbler—A large tumbler in blue and representing a basket weave.

Shell Footed Creamer — Here is a large creamer showing shell feet and scalloped top. It is shown in blue here.

Mosaic Creamer   Basket Weave Tumbler   Shell Footed Creamer

PLATE 210

Sawtooth Butter   Sawtooth Master Salt   Sawtooth Compote

PLATE 211

Sawtooth Creamer   Sawtooth Spooner   Sawtooth Celery Holder

PLATE 212

Sawtooth Butter, Master Salt, High Compote, Creamer, Spooner and Celery Holder—It is not known what firm made this pattern but it is one of the oldest in milk white glass. It is getting quite scarce for the good pieces and will soon demand high prices. It is to be had in most pieces for a set except the goblets and plates. It was made during the 60's.

Stippled Forget-me-not Creamer, Celery Holder And Tumbler—A pattern much sought and getting scarce. It is not known who made it but it is thought the earlier pieces were Sandwich made. The type of glass in the early milk white pieces would suggest this is a probability but there is no data confirming this thought. The milk white pieces are getting scarce and are now quite difficult to pick up. It is collectable in sets except plates. It is supposed to be a pattern developed in the early 80's.

Stippled Forget-me-not Creamer, Celery Holder and Tumbler

PLATE 213

Cosmos Open Sugar   Crown Covered Sugar

PLATE 214

Apple Blossom Covered Sugar   Swan Covered Sugar

PLATE 215

Cosmos Open Sugar—A piece of this well known pattern and in this case there seems to have been no cover. As usual it is an attractive piece and is collectable in sets.

Crown Covered Sugar—A rather large sugar with a crown on the cover, and in most instances painted on the scroll like elements.

Apple Blossom Covered Sugar—A bulb shaped sugar with beaded creas-es above and below. It is painted on most of the surface.

Swan Covered Sugar—An attractive sugar with swan necks for handles and a small swan on the cover as a finial.

Shell Pattern Set—A set of covered sugar, creamer, handled mug and spooner is shown here. It is a very white set and makes an attractive setting. All pieces are footed, and handled.

Shell Pattern Set

PLATE 216

Northwood Water Pitcher   Scroll Tankard   Water Lily Water Pitcher

PLATE 217

Pansy Bottle   Classic Footed Water Pitcher   Covered Stein

PLATE 218

Northwood Water Pitcher—A large water pitcher of this well known pattern, in custard glass. It is 3 quarts.

Scroll Tankard—A very tall tankard of this well known pattern.

Water Lily Water Pitcher—A bulbous type pitcher with water lillies on the body of the piece. It is a 4 quart pitcher.

Pansy Bottle—A covered bottle with large pansies on the sides and a large stopper.

Classic Footed Water Pitcher—A rare piece in this pattern, which is scarce for any piece and exceptionally for the water pitcher. It was made by The Portland Glass Co., during the 70's.

Covered Stein—A rather low type of stein, with the bust of a lady. It is covered as usual.

Diamond Flute Pink Creamer—An unusual footed creamer both in color and shape. It is footed and is a rich pink color of marble glass.

Metal Handle Syrup—A medium sized syrup with bulb bowl and scrolled. It is painted and has a metal handle.

Cream Colored Sundae—A flute type of sundae with scalloped top and of a cream color.

Strawberry Open Vase—A bulb shaped vase with large strawberries and leaves on the body.

Diamond Flute Pink Creamer   Metal Handle Syrup   Cream Colored Sundae   Strawberry Open Vase

PLATE 219

Marble Glass Platter   Marble Glass Lattice Plate

PLATE 220

Marble Glass Notched Edged Tray   Marble Glass Flowered Water Pitcher

PLATE 221

Marble Glass Platter—A heavy piece of purple glass measuring 10 inches long. It is plain on the surface and very heavy.

Marble Glass Lattice Plate—A large lattice edge plate with the usual swirl-like centre. It is an Atterbury piece made during the 80's. It is 12 inches.

Marble Glass Notched Edge Tray —A large tray in the purple glass with large dots in the centre and a well notched edge. It is 9 by 12½ inches.

Marble Glass Flowered Water Pitcher—A large pitcher of purple glass in which the white predominates.

Liberty Bell Mug—A small mug with the liberty bell on the side.

Corset Match Holder—This piece was made to represent a corset and is a match holder.

Marble Glass, Small Creamer—A small creamer with rich colors in the purple marble glass.

Bible Match Holder—A match holder in the shape of the bible.

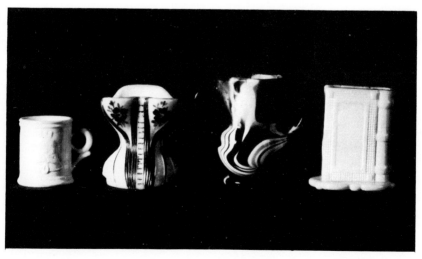

| Liberty
Bell Mug | Corset Match
Holder | Marble Glass, Small
Creamer | Bible Match
Holder |

PLATE 222

Marble Compote, Basket Stem   Marble Ribbed Compote

PLATE 223

Marble Hexagon Sugar   Marble Fluted Butter   Marble Beaded Tumbler

PLATE 224

Marble Compote, Basket Stem—A very desirable piece in the purple marble glass. This piece is also found in the yellow or golden marble shade. It is 7 inches tall and 9 inches across the top.

Marble Ribbed Compote—A tall compote in the purple marble shade with ribbing all over the body and stem. It is 8½ inches tall and 8¾ inches wide.

Marble Hexagon Sugar—A small sugar or possibly a marmalade jar in hexagon shape with a knob finial cover.

Marble Fluted Butter—A large covered butter in the fluted pattern which is so often met with in the purple marble glass. This piece measures 8½ inches tall and 8¼ inches wide.

Marble Beaded Tumbler—A dark tumbler in the purple glass with fine beading on the bowl and panelled with bars.

Marble Square Set—Here is a set of square purple marble glass with an oval medallion on each piece. The coloring is very outstanding and pleasing, with much white.

Marble Square Set

PLATE 225

Marble Crown Top Sugar   Marble Lattice Water Pitcher   Marble Crown Top Spooner

PLATE 226

Marble Ribbed Jelly Dish   Marble Fluted Celery   Marble Tripod Flower Vase

PLATE 227

Marble Crown Top Sugar—A large sugar with a crown on the cover and a shell like design on the lower part of the bowl. It is very highly colored.

Marble Lattice Water Pitcher—A rather dark water pitcher with practically all the surface covered by fine lattice work on the surface. It is 10 inches high.

Marble Crown Top Spooner—A spooner which matches the sugar opposite on this cut. It is a richly colored piece.

Marble Ribbed Jelly Dish—A large and darkly colored dish with plain stem. It is an open top piece.

Marble Fluted Celery—A very tall celery holder with rich colors predominating. It is 9 inches tall.

Marble Tripod Flower Vase—A tripod, legged vase with wide lip and an upturned flange on the edge.

Marble Fluted Oblong Tray—A large tray with handles on either end and scalloped edges. It is highly colored.

Marble Scalloped Nappie—A large nappie with six scallops and a ruffled edge. It was made at Greentown, Indiana.

Marble Fluted Oblong Tray   Marble Scalloped Nappie

PLATE 228

Marble Beaded Celery   Marble Cat's Eye Vase   Marble Round Bowl Goblet

PLATE 229

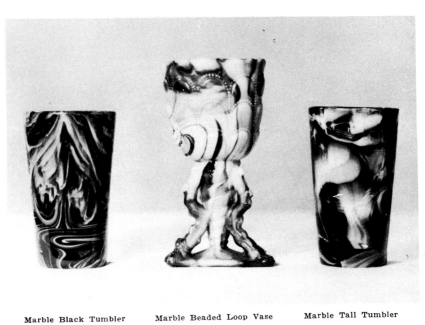

Marble Black Tumbler   Marble Beaded Loop Vase   Marble Tall Tumbler

PLATE 230

Marble Beaded Celery—A tall, narrow celery holder with band of beads around the bowl. It is 8 inches tall.

Marble Cat's Eye Vase—A rustic type of vase with tree limbs for legs to a flat base. The body is covered with cat's eyes. It is 8½ inches tall.

Marble Round Bowl Goblet—This goblet is shown here as it is a differing shape and more highly colored than any shown in the goblet books. It is rare.

Marble Black Tumbler—A very darkish, in fact almost black, tumbler with intricate white linings thru the coloring.

Marble Beaded Loop Vase—A rather tall vase with beaded loops over the body and with tripod legs to a flat base. It is 9 inches tall.

Marble Tall Tumbler—A very highly colored and tall tumbler in the purple marble glass.

Marble Creased Bowl—A large oval shaped bowl with deep creases in the body making it appear as coarse ribbed. It is 7 inches tall.

Marble Square Soap Dish—A very heavy dish in very highly colored mixture.

Marble Creased Bowl   Marble Square Soap Dish

PLATE 231

Marble Round Lip Mug   Marble Square Match   **Marble Flower Mug**

PLATE 232

Marble Rib Footed Dish   **Marble, Pink Mug**   **Marble Ring Handle Match**

PLATE 233

Marble Glass Round Lip Mug—A medium sized mug in the purple glass. Most of this type of glass was made by the Indiana Tumbler And Goblet Co., of Greeentown, Indiana.

Square Marble Glass Match Holder—A tall match holder of the purple glass mixture.

Marble Glass, Flowered Mug—A large mug, covered with flowers, made in a rich mixture of purple glass.

Marble Glass Rib Footed Dish—A small dish in dark purple glass and with handles on each side.

Marble Glass, Pink, Mug—A large mug with square handle and of deep pink color. Undoubtedly a trial piece as few of them are seen.

Marble Glass, Ring Handle, Match—A slender and rather tall match holder of dark purple. It has rings on each side.

Marble Glass, Heavy Footed Bowl—A very heavy bowl footed, and in very light colored mixture. It is 6 inches tall, 6 inches wide and 10 inches long.

Double Head Chick—The usual chick with a small head near the tail. This is an unusual piece, for two heads to appear on one piece.

Marble Heavy, Footed Bowl   Double Head Chick

PLATE 234

Marble Double
Handle Tumbler

Marble Octagon
Tumbler

Marble, Green
Swirl Tumbler

PLATE 235

Black, Bee
Match

Black Turtle

Marble Handled
Master Salt

Marble, Handled
Match

PLATE 236

Marble Glass Double Handle Tumbler—A tall tumbler with large outstanding handles on each side.

Marble Glass Octagon Tumbler—A tall and rather heavy tumbler of a very light color in purple glass.

Marble Glass, Green, Swirl Tumbler—A medium sized tumbler which is deep green in color. This color is rare and hard to find. It has a flower covered body.

Black Bee Match Holder—A small match holder in black glass, with bees on the sides.

Black Turtle—A large turtle in the black glass with head near the surface. It has a cover. It is probably a British piece.

Marble Glass Handled Master Salt—A master salt in rich color and handled.

Marble Glass, Handled, Match Holder—A rather small match holder of a light colored piece.

Marble Glass Hen—An 8 inch hen of the purple glass type which is one of the rarest pieces in purple glass.

Colored Duck—An 8 inch duck on a white base but with painted body.

Marble Glass Hen   Colored Duck

PLATE 237

Caramel Dolphin   PLATE 238   Caramel Hen

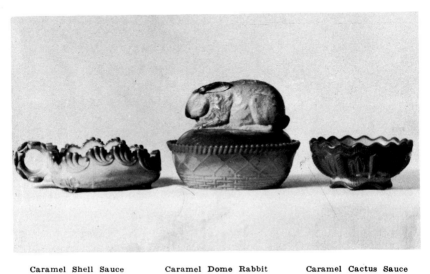

Caramel Shell Sauce   Caramel Dome Rabbit   Caramel Cactus Sauce

PLATE 239

Caramel Dolphin—A dolphin dish with cover showing a small fish on the lid. It was made by the Indiana Tumbler And Goblet Co., of Greentown, -Indiana.

Caramel Hen—Here is the usual sized small hen in caramel glass color. The details of the tail feathers are deeply cut. It is a Greentown, Indiana product. 5¼ inches long.

Caramel Shell Sauce—A rather heavy, handled sauce with shell design near the top.

Caramel Dome Rabbit—Another piece made by Greentown, Indiana and is 5½ inches long.

Caramel Cactus Sauce—A small sauce with cactus pattern on the sides. It is also a Greentown product.

Caramel Beaded Rib Mug—A heavy handled mug with beaded ribs on the sides. It is of Greentown manufacture.

Caramel Shell Sugar—A covered sugar with the shell pattern and a ball finial on the lid. It is a product of Greentown, Indiana.

Caramel, Dewey Creamer — A creamer in the pattern called "Dewey" by the Indiana Tumbler & Goblet Co., of Greentown, Indiana.

Caramel Beaded Rib Mug   Caramel Shell Sugar   Caramel Dewey Creamer

PLATE 240

Caramel Cactus Tumbler   Caramel Cactus Mug   Caramel Cord Drapery Tumbler

PLATE 241

Caramel Cactus Salt and Pepper   Caramel Cactus Coffee Urn

PLATE 242

Caramel Cactus Tumbler—A tumbler in the cactus pattern. Be it remembered that the Indiana Tumbler And Goblet Co., of Greentown, Ind. made the major portion of caramel glass. They are early 1900.

Caramel Cactus Mug—A large mug with handle elevated from the horizontal.

Caramel Cord Drapery Tumbler—Here is a caramel tumbler of the usual cord drapery pattern.

Caramel Cactus Salt And Pepper—This pair of condiments in the caramel glass pattern of cactus is a very attractive set.

Caramel Cactus Coffee Urn—This medium sized coffee urn in the cactus pattern of caramel glass is a very outstanding piece and is hard to find.

Caramel Chickens Cover—A 5½ inch covered dish with a pair of fighting chickens on the cover. It is rare.

Caramel Oblong Pickle — This piece shows the bottom as it is figured while the inside is plain.

Caramel Chickens Cover   Caramel Oblong Pickle

PLATE 243

Northwood Custard Set, Unmarked
PLATE 244

Northwood Set, Marked
PLATE 245

Northwood Custard Set, Unmarked —A set of this pattern which does not have the signature on the bottom. Be it remembered that there were sets made without this signature.

Northwood Creamer—A creamer of the marked set. These patterns all are made in blue and custard.

Northwood Covered S u g a r—A large sugar of this pattern marked.

Northwood Custard Spooner—This piece is also marked and all above are in the custard color.

Northwood Footed Sauce—This sauce has scroll feet and the scrolls extend upon the sides. It is in blue.

Scalloped Edge Nappie—A large nappie with scalloped top and a hole for hanging. It is hexagon in outline.

Northwood Sauce, Scalloped Top —A footed sauce which has scalloped top and of the usual pattern on the body. It is custard color.

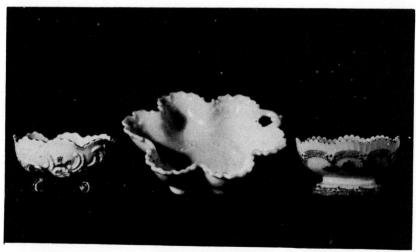

Northwood Footed   Scalloped Edge Nappie   Northwood Sauce,
Sauce, Blue   Scalloped Top

PLATE 246

Northwood Shell
Sauce

Northwood Shell
Compote

Northwood Shell
Sauce

PLATE 247

Spider-webb Lamp

Beaded Medallion Lamp

PLATE 248

Northwood Shell Sauces—These sauces are very attractive and rather hard to find. They are a well marked shell pattern and are custard color.

Northwood Compote—A large compote of the shell pattern in custard glass which is getting scarce and much sought by collectors recently.

Spider-webb Lamp—A large lamp with low bulged bowl and a large globe showing the spider-webb pattern to advantage. It is scarce.

Beaded Medallion Lamp—A lamp in blue, which shows multiple medallions, enclosing a daisy. It has a reeded stem.

Basket Match Holder—A match holder in the shape of a small handled basket. It is blue.

Children Match Holder—An oblong match holder with two children sitting on a bench. It is blue in color.

Fluer de Lis Match Holder—A match holder in the shape of a Fluer de Lis. It is blue.

Basket Toothpick Holder—A small basket toothpick holder. It is white.

| Basket Match | Children Match | Fleur de Lis | Basket Toothpick |
| Holder | Holder | Match Holder | Holder |

PLATE 248—A

Daisy And Scroll Lamp   Beaded Loop Lamp   Octagon Medallion Lamp

PLATE 249

Bulbed Scroll
Lamp   Fleur de Lis
Lamp   Swan Lamp   Roman Key
Lamp

PLATE 250

Daisy And Scroll Lamp—A slender lamp with daisies interspered with heavy scroll.

Beaded Loop Lamp—This lamp shows a beaded band on the bowl and flue. It is rather attractive and desirable.

Octagon Medallion Lamp—T h e bowl and flue both show medallions in an octagon shape. It is rather tall.

Bulbed Scroll Lamp—A scroll type lamp with a low bulb on the bowl and the same on the flue.

Fluer de Lis Lamp—The bulbous bowl and flue both show Fluer de Lis as panels.

Swan Lamp—As the name would indicate, the body represents a swan swimming.

Roman Key Lamp—A small lamp of the boudoir type with a band of Roman key around the bowl and flue.

Wire Handle Lamp—A plain white bowl with clear flue and a wire handle, which is double at the handle and surrounding the bowl.

Eagle And Arrows Lamp—A large bulbous lamp and flue, both showing a spread wing eagle and arrows in the feet.

Panelled Scalloped Lamp—A tall, slender lamp with scallops on the bowl and flue.

Wire Handled Lamp   Eagle And Arrows Lamp   Panelled Scalloped Lamp

PLATE 251

Beaded Loop Lamp,   Cosmos Lamp   Bulb Whale   Block And
No Flue, Blue   Oil Lamp   Circle Lamp

PLATE 252

Double Creased   Pot Bulbed   Pear Shaped   Block Lamp
Lamp   Lamp   Lamp

PLATE 253

Beaded Loop Lamp, No Flue—A lamp the same as plate 249 with the exception that the flue is missing and it is in blue.

Cosmos Lamp—A pattern shown in many pieces and here as a lamp. It is always painted.

Bulb Whale Oil Lamp—A whale oil lamp with round foot and a bulbous body. It has flowers painted on the sides.

Block And Circle Lamp—A small lamp of the block type, with a circular dot in each panel, of an octagon shape.

Double Creased Lamp—A small lamp with creases below and above. It has a rural scene painted on.

Pot Bulbed Lamp—A lamp with a large pot bulbed type of bowl, which is painted. A clear flue.

Pear Shaped Lamp—The body of this lamp shows a pear shaped body, which is painted. A clear flue.

Block Lamp — A small boudoir lamp with both body and flue in the block type.

Creased Bulb Lamp—A large, flat type of bowl. Both body and flue show perpendicular crease and thus the outline is bulbed.

Panelled Fluer de Lis Lamp—A large bowl lamp with octagon shape and on each division point a large Fluer de Lis is conspicious.

Rose Scroll Lamp—A tall, slender lamp of lobular type with large roses forming scrolls on the body and flue.

Creased Bulb Lamp   Panelled Fleur de Lis Lamp   Rose Scroll Lamp

PLATE 254

Ringed Flat Lamp   Footed Pyramid Lamp

PLATE 255

Flare Bottom Lamp   Scroll Lamp

PLATE 256

Ringed Flat Lamp—A large bowled lamp of a flat type with rings above and below on the bowl.

Footed Pyramid Lamp—A tapering shaped body lamp showing an offset above the foot.

Flare Bottom Lamp—A very large flare bottom type of lamp with circular foot, and scrolls around the base.

Scroll Lamp—A very large lamp with heavy scrolls on the bowl and a metallic foot.

Pink whale Oil Lamp—A rare whale oil lamp in deep pink color. It has a tall foot and slender body, in octagon shape.

Square Candle Holder—A tall candle holder in white with rings around the stem.

Hexagon Base Lamp—A large lamp showing a hexagon base and stem with leaf scrolls on the foot, top and bottom of the bowl. The bowl is square, thus a peculiar shape.

Pink Whale Oil Lamp   Square Candle Holder   Hexagon Base Lamp

PLATE 257

Winter Scene Lamp   Fern And Scroll Lamp

PLATE 258

Victoria Covered Jar   Coin Lamp

PLATE 259

Winter Scene Lamp—A large lamp with a squarish bowl and metal foot. It has a painted scene of Winter on the bowl.

Fern And Scroll Lamp—A very large bulbous type of lamp with heavy scroll and ferns on the body. It has a metal foot.

Victoria Covered Jar—A covered jar with Queen Victoria on the lid and the inscription on the sides of the body.

Coin Lamp—An example of a rare lamp in this much sought pattern.

Square Stem Lamp, Pink—A pink lamp of medium size with a square foot and stem.

Dark Blue Lamp—Here is a rare lamp of dark blue. It shows a ribbed body and scalloped foot, which is deep pink in color.

Pinion Stem Lamp—A pink lamp with the pinion foot to be placed in a candle holder or other suitable holder. It is rare.

Square Stem Lamp, Pink   Dark Blue Lamp   Pinion Stem Lamp

PLATE 260

Purple Overlay Lamp   Pink Bowl Lamp   Green Overlay Lamp

PLATE 261

Square, Pink Bowl Lamp   School-house Lamp   Pink Overlay Lamp

PLATE 262

Purple Overlay Lamp—Here is an overlay lamp with purple over the clear glass. It has a stepped white foot. It is a rare lamp.

Pink Bowl Lamp—A flat type of bowl in pink and a large square white base with metal connector.

Green Overlay Lamp—Another lamp of the overlay type which is white over green. It shows a square white base and metal connector. It is also rare.

Square Pink Lamp—Here is a square bowl lamp with lobulated flue and both are in a rich rose pink. It is rare.

School-house Lamp—A small night lamp, with applied handle, in the shape of a school-house. It is rare.

Pink Overlay Lamp—Another overlay lamp with white over pink. It has a large marble foot and a metal stem. It is rare.

Ring Handled Vase — A large ribbed vase with ring handles on each side. It shows panels of leaves also. It is rare.

Pleated Bowl Marble Glass Lamp —A tall lamp with a white pleated bowl and a marble glass foot and stem. It is a rare lamp.

Grape Water Pitcher—A large water pitcher of this well known pattern. It is unusual to find these large water pitchers in Grape pattern.

Ring Handled Vase   Pleated Bowl, Marble Glass Lamp   Grape Water Pitcher

PLATE 263

Tulip Petal Lamp   Clock Lamp   Beaded Bulb Lamp

PLATE 264

Doric Column Lamp   Scroll Foot Lamp   Plain Boudoir Lamp

PLATE 265

Tulip Petal Lamp—A small lamp with tulip petals forming the body and with a clear flue. It is unusual to find.

Clock Lamp—A rare lamp with large bowl and massive, square foot. It has an octagon stem with a small clock insert. It is blue. It is very rare.

Beaded Bulb Lamp—A small lamp of lobular, bulbed type of bowl and a perpendicular line of beads between each lobule.

Doric Column Lamp—A tall lamp in white with doric stem. It has a beaded scroll foot.

Scroll Foot Lamp—A very large lamp with heavy scroll foot. It also shows scrolls on the body. It is hard to find.

Plain Boudoir Lamp—A medium sized lamp with plain, flat bowl, and a rounded foot and stem.

Candy Stripe Lamp—A rare lamp with white foot of the stepped type. It has a candy stripe type of bowl. It is rare.

Twin Student Lamp—A double bowl student lamp with frosted flues and white foot and bowls. It has a metal connector. It is rare.

Candy Stripe Lamp   Twin Student Lamp

PLATE 266

Blue Head Hen. Lacy Dish   Brown Marble Hen, Lacy Edge Dish

PLATE 267

Boar Head   Yellow Marble Hen, Basket Dish

PLATE 268

Marble Hens On Lacy Edge Bases —All of the hen dishes on these pages were produced by Atterbury & Co., of Pittsburg, Pa. One shows a basket weave base, which is proper. The other three are all on lacy edge bases. The variations in color, especially on their backs, does not show in photographs because blue makes white photos. They constitute a very attractive assortment in colors. These hens have the head turned to one side in uniform attitude. They are all 8 inch dishes. This assortment is difficult to find and are becoming scarcer every year. All have glass eyes.

The Boar Head—A covered dish made by Atterbury & Co., is placed on a ribbed base. It is of rather heavy material and has glass eyes. It is getting scarce and is a very desirable collector's piece.

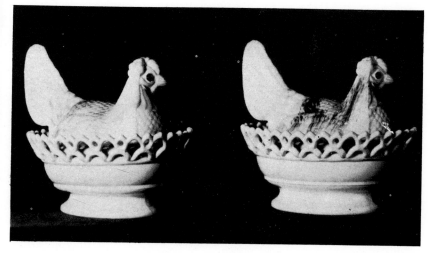

White Hen, On Lacy Edge Dish   Blue Marble Hen, Lacy Edge Dish

PLATE 269

Duck, Ribbed Base   Straight Head Hen

PLATE 270

Pin Tail Duck   Grass Base Duck

PLATE 271

Duck, Ribbed Base—A very pleasing type of covered duck dish with glass eyes and is 8½ inches long. It is on a ribbed base.

Straight Head Hen—Another Atterbury piece in the 8 inch size. The Hen's head is almost straight ahead in this instance. It belongs on a lacy edge base, and has glass eyes.

Pin Tail Duck—A 5½ inch covered dish with a stub tailed duck on cover. The base is a split rib type. It is a Westmoreland product.

Grass Base Duck—A 5½ inch duck covered dish with a grass base and is a rich opalescent piece.

Swimming Duck—This piece has a footed base and forms a part of the body. It is 6 inches long and has the head raised in a peculiar manner.

Basket Base Duck—A 6½ inch duck rests on a basket base which is the proper base.

Swimming Duck　　　　　Basket Base Duck

PLATE 272

Large Rooster and Hen
PLATE 273

Black Hen   Black Hen With White Head
PLATE 274

Large Rooster And Hen—This particular pair show glass eyes and are both white. There are several made in this 8 inch size and some do not have glass eyes. They are made in white, blue, painted to represent dominecker chickens. They all rest on basket weave bases. The fowls with glass eyes are among the older patterns.

Small Hen And Rooster Dishes—These fowls in 5½ inch dishes are various as to color combinations. The roosters should be on ribbed bases while the hens all rest on basket bases. The combinations of colors seen are as follows: white, white with blue head, blue with white head, blue, black, black with white head, clear amber glass with white head. There are many varieties of crystal glass combinations in color made in recent years. Most of the small white hens are foreign made, mostly Japanese.

Blue Hen and Rooster
PLATE 275

Straight Back Rooster   Swan Salt

PLATE 276

Owl Milk Pitcher   Large Swan

PLATE 277

Straight Back Rooster—Here is an entirely differing rooster on a rib base. The head and tail are raised high and the back low. It is a 5½ inch piece, on a ribbed base.

Swan Salt—An attractive salt which is 5 inches long. It is a Sandwich piece and shows the excellent type of glass characteristic of this factory.

Owl Milk Pitcher—This piece is 8 inches tall and has glass eyes. It is a product of Atterbury & Co., and was created during the early 80's. It comes in white and blue colors.

Large Swan—A large covered dish with a swan for the cover. It has no glass eyes ordinarily. The base is ribbed and is 10 inches long. It is an Atterbury product, also during the 80's.

Closed Neck Swan—A small covered dish with a 5½ inch swan for the cover. The neck is closed. It rests on a split rib base.

Open Neck Swan—Another 5½ inch dish with swan for cover. It has an open neck and rests on a split rib base. It is a McKee Brothers piece.

Closed Neck Swan   Open Neck Swan

PLATE 278

Swan With Raised Wings, Lacy Edge Dish   Tomato Dish

PLATE 279

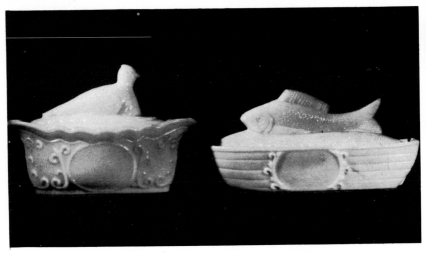

Quail Cover   Fish Cover

PLATE 280

Swan With Raised Wings—A large swan by the Atterbury Co., on a lacy edge dish. It is scarce. It measures 6 inches by 9½ inches long.

Tomato Dish—A covered dish in the shape of a tomato. It is 6 inches in diameter and is scarce.

Quail Cover—A quail cover rests on a scroll base. It is of the 5½ inch dimensions. It is hard to find.

Fish Cover—An elongated dish with a fish as cover. It is 7½ inches long and boat shaped.

Large Swan On Basket Base—An 8 inch swan in blue on a basket base. It is of the closed neck variety and this size is hard to find.

Medium Sized Swan—This swan is 9 inches in diameter and is on a block base. It is getting scarce. Made by Atterburuy & Co., during the 80's.

Eight Inch Swan, Blue   Nine Inch Swan

PLATE 281

Robed Santa Claus
On Sleigh

Dome Sheep Cover

Standing Bear

PLATE 282

Hen On Sleigh

Santa Claus On Sleigh

PLATE 283

Robed Santa Claus On Sleigh—A small sleigh with a Santa Claus robed. It is a 5½ inch piece.

Dome Sheep—A small sheep rests on a dome base. It is a Flaccus piece and is scarce. It is 6 inches long.

Standing Bear—A muzzled bear in a standing position and resembling an organ grinder's bear. It is 6 inches tall.

Hen On Sleigh—A small hen on a 5½ inch sleigh. By the Westmorland Co.

Santa Claus On Sleigh—A Santa Claus with a taboggin on his head. It is a 5½ inch peice.

Dove Cover—A 5½ inch dish with a dove as a cover. It is a McKee piece and is scarce.

Chick In Egg On Sleigh—A chick's head protrudes from an egg which rests in a sleigh. It is a 5½ inch piece. A Westmorland product.

Dove Cover   Chick In Egg On Sleigh

PLATE 284

Owl Jelly Jar   Pedestal Rooster   Eagle Covered Jar

PLATE 285

Moses In The Bull Rushes   Turkey Cover

PLATE 286

Owl Jelly Jar—A small owl jar with glass eyes. It is an Atterbury Co., product of the 80's.

Pedestal Rooster — This covered dish is the body of a rooster which rests on a footed pedestal. It is a rather scarce piece to find.

Eagle Covered Jar—A jar with the shape of the body of an eagle, resting on a circular base.

Moses In The Bull Rushes—A 5½ inch piece of very strikingly opalescent character and a grass base. It is hard to find.

Turkey Cover—A 5½ inch dish, with a turkey on top. It rests on a split rib base. It is getting scarce and hard to find. The quality of the glass is excellent in this piece.

White Rooster And Hen—A pair of white fowls made by the Westmorland Speciality Co., of Grapeville, Pa., and only here shown to illustrate their type.

White Rooster and Hen
PLATE 287

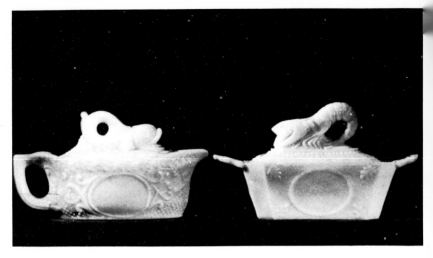

Dolphin Cover   Crawfish Top

PLATE 288

Fish Covered Dish   Robin On Pedestal Nest

PLATE 289

Dolphin Cover—A 7¼ inch dish with a dolphin on the cover. It has a special base and has been attributed to The Westmorland Co. It is a gravy or syrup dish, with a long spout.

Crawfish Top—This piece has an old fashioned crawfish on the cover. It is 7½ inches long and has a special squarish base, with handles.

Fish Covered Dish—Here is a dish entirely composed of the body of a fish. It has glass eyes and rests on the fins for feet. It is a Challinor, Taylor & Co., product of the 80's.

Robin On Pedestal Nest—A cov-ered dish with robin on cover, resting on a footed pedestal and a nest like bowl. It was made at Greentown, Indiana.

Cherry Sugar—A covered sugar of square outline with cherries on the panels. It has a twig for a finial top. A Bakewell, Pears Co. product.

Hen On Chick Base—Here is a 6¼ inch covered dish on a specially decorated base with chicks running around the area. It is a Flaccus piece.

Ring Handled Mug—A handled mug with ring handles which show rounded knobs above and below on the rings. It has a swan on the sides.

Cherry Sugar   Hen On Chick Base   Ring Handled Mug

PLATE 290

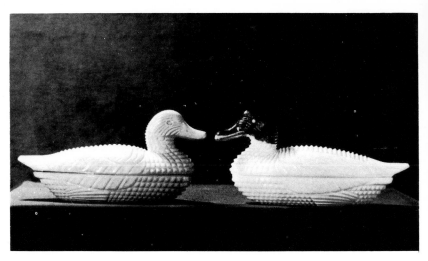

Blue Duck   Duck With Amethyst Head

PLATE 291

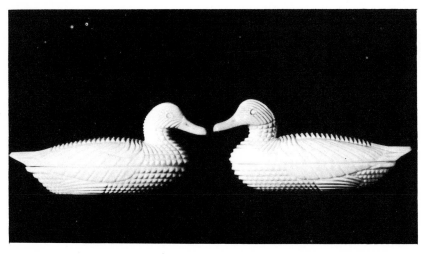

White Duck   White Duck With Blue Head

PLATE 292

A color combination of large 11 inch ducks, which show blue, white with amethyst colored head, white, white with blue head, and the patent which was granted the Atterbury Co., for its manufactory. The amethyst colored head is said to be the rarest of milk white covered dishes extant. There are suitable eye orbits for insertion of glass eyes, but these have not had them inserted. They were created during the late 80's. Prices have steadily risen on these pieces until now they are considered scarce. This entire collection belongs to Dr. Frank Patterson, of Hunter, Oklahoma, and was through his generosity and kindness they were loaned for these photos.

Patent For Duck Design

PLATE 293

Chick And Egg On Basket

Indian Head Match

PLATE 294

Dewey, Scroll Base

Uncle Tom Cigar Holder

"Mammy" On a Wash Tub

PLATE 295

Chick And Egg On Basket—This piece shows a basket with handles and a chick emerging from an egg on the cover. A Westmorland piece.

Indian Head Match—A match holder intended to be hung on the wall. It shows a feather decked head of an Indian.

Dewey, Scroll Base—Here is a small casket like base with the bust of Admiral Dewey as a cover.

Uncle Tom Cigar Holder—A cup like cigar holder with an old negro's face and head as the body. It is old.

Mammy On A Wash Tub—A tub like base with an old negro mammy's bust as the cover. It is hard to find.

The American Hen — A spread wing eagle on an oblong base with the characteristic inscription on the sides.

Dewey, Tile Base—Here is another casket type of base, in tile, with the bust of Admiral Dewey on the cover. It is a much longer piece than the former one shown and thus entirely different. It is very desirable.

The American Hen   Dewey, Tile Base

PLATE 296

Little Red School House   Dewey, Patriotic Base

PLATE 297

Bull's Head Mustard   Owl Head Cover

PLATE 298

Little Red School House—This piece represents a school house and is painted brick like. It has a slot in the chimmey for insertion of coins and is thus a penny bank. It was made by the Westmorland Specialty Co., of Grapeville, Pa.

Dewey, Patrotic Base—Here is another bust of Admiral Dewey on a patriotic type of casket with the Coat of Arms and crossed cannon. It is of fine material.

Bull's Head Mustard—An opalescent bull's head with the ladle serving as the tongue. It is an Atterbury Product.

Owl Head Cover—A covered dish with an owl head on a split rib base. It is an Atterbury Co., production during the 80's.

Plain Bulging Bottle—Here is a bottle with a narrow neck and a great bulging base. It is plain in outline.

Dewey, Round Ribbed Base—Still another type of the bust of Admiral Dewey on a ribbed base. This piece is of small dimensions. It was made at Greentown, Indiana.

Plain Bulging Bottle   Dewey, Round Ribbed Base

PLATE 299

Battleship Maine   Cruiser Ship

PLATE 300

Kettle Drum Cannon   Snare Drum Cannon

PLATE 301

Battleship Maine—A covered dish representing the Battleship Maine, the flagship of Admiral Dewey. It is 7 inches long.

Cruiser Ship—Another boat type of covered dish measuring 7½ inches long. It represents the type of sh.p used during The Spanish American war.

Kettle Drum Cannon—A kettle drum base with a cannon and grape on the cover. It represents the type of cannon used during the civil war.

Snare Drum Cannon—Another of the drum type of base with a similar cannon on the cover. It is also characteristic of the civil war.

Leaf Edge Plate, Blue—Another of this pattern but in the blue. It is a 10 inch plate with deep bowl.

Panelled Hobnail Plate—A 6 inch plate of this well known pattern but with the design on the bottom of the plate. The face of the plate is plain.

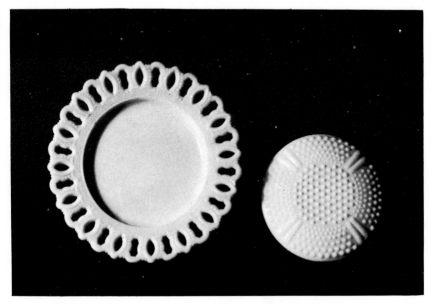

Leaf Edge Plate, Blue   Panelled Hobnail Plate

PLATE 302

Horse Cover   Cow Cover

PLATE 303

Small Elephant Cover   Lion, Split Rib Base

PLATE 304

Horse Cover—This is a very desirable piece and hard to find. They are bringing higher prices than formerly. It is a McKee Brothers piece. It rests on a split rib base only.

Cow Cover—Here is another of the animal covered dishes with a cow lying on the cover. It is an opalescent piece which is becoming scarce. It rests on a split rib base.

Small Elephant Cover—Here is an elephant, with lowered trunk, on the cover of a 5½ inch base dish. It belongs on a split rib base.

Lion, Split Rib Base—A recumbent lion on a 5½ inch base which is a split rib. It is a very desirable piece by the McKee Brothers.

Lion, Scroll Base—A lion lying on a scroll base which is 5¾ inches long and is square.

Lion, Ribbed Base—A lion with head turned to one side and resting on a coarse ribbed base. It is 5½ inches long and the base is octagon in outline.

Lion, Scroll Base   Lion, Ribbed Base

PLATE 305

Lacy Edged Hen And Eggs   Lacy Edged Fox

PLATE 306

Lacy Edged Cat   Ribbed Dish Lion

PLATE 307

Lacy Edged Hen And Eggs—A large 8 inch lacy edged base with a hen on eggs which protrude above her body. It is an Atterbury & Co. piece of the 80's.

Lacy Edged Fox—Another of the 8 inch lacy edged dishes with a recumbent fox on the cover. It is an Atterbury piece created, as the one above, in the late 80's.

Lacy Edged Cat—A large cat on an 8 inch lacy edged dish, created by Atterbury during the 80's.

Ribbed Dish Lion—A large recumbent lion rests on an 8 inch dish which is ribbed on the base and cover. It is a 7½ inch piece made by Atterbury & Co., during the 80's.

British Lion—A large lion resting on a figured base with "The British Lion" inscription. It is a 6¼ inch piece.

Fish Pickle—A waffle type pickle dish, 9 inches long in the form of a large cubed fish, with eyes. It was created by Challinor, Taylor & Co., of Tarentum, Pa.

British Lion   Fish Pickle, Waffle Type

PLATE 308

Hart On Fallen Tree Base   Uncle Sam Battleship

PLATE 309

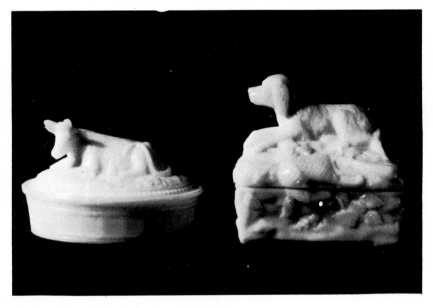

Cow On Round Base   Setter On Square Base

PLATE 310

Hart, On A Fallen Tree Base—A finely made, opalescent piece by The Flaccus Co., which measures 6¾ inches long. It rests on a base showing a fallen tree and other foilage.

Uncle Sam Battleship—A battleship 6¾ inches long with "Uncle Sam" sitting on the cover. It is a Flaccus piece.

Cow On Round Base—A cow in a recumbent position and on a round base. It is very opalescent in color and is a Vallerystall or French piece. It is 5¾ inches long.

Setter On Square Base—A nice piece showing a Gordon setter resting on the cover of a rough, square base. It measures 6½ inches long and is a Flaccus piece.

Squirrel Cover—A 5½ inch piece showing a recumbent squirrel on the cover. It rests on a split rib base and is a McKee piece.

Pomeranian Dog Cover—A small dog resting on the cover of a square dish of lattice design. It measures 3½ inches by 4¾ inches on the base. It is scarce.

Squirrel Cover   Pomeranian Dog Cover

PLATE 311

Mule Eared Rabbit   PLATE 312   Flat Eared Rabbit

Turtle Cover   PLATE 313   Dome Rabbit

Mule Eared Rabbit—A 5½ inch piece with upright ears on the rabbit. It rests on an octagon, ribbed base.

Flat Eared Rabbit—A McKee piece resting on a 5½ inch split ribbed base. It is getting to be a rather rare, and is of fine opalescent hue.

Turtle Cover—A turtle rests on the cover of a dish (with handles) and with scroll and circle outline. It measures 7 inches over all. It is not plentiful.

Dome Rabbit—A recumbent rabbit resting on a domed shape cover and with split ribbed base. It is a piece produced at Greentown, Ind.

Square Basket With Chicks—A small piece measuring 2½ by 4¼ inches in diameter and on a basket weave base.

Beaver Cover—A beaver with humped back rests on a diamond checked base. It is hard to find. It is 5½ inches long.

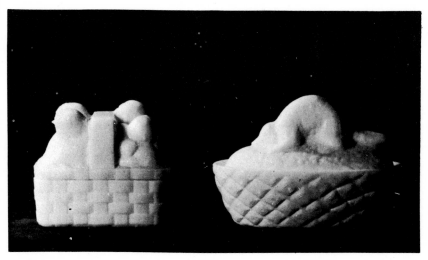

Square Basket With Chicks   Beaver Cover

PLATE 314

Camel, Lying   Elephant

PLATE 315

Lamb, Ribbed Base   Lamb, Hexagon Base

PLATE 316

Camel Lying—Here is a piece with the entire dish representing the body of the camel. It is a British piece and is here shown as it is being ardently collected.

Elephant—A large 9 inch elephant with the trunk uplifted. It is also a British piece and is being sought by collectors.

Lamb, Ribbed Base—A lamb resting on a rib base, which was made by McKee Brothers. It is 5½ inches long.

Lamb, Octagon Base—A wooly lamb rests on an octagon base of the coarse rib type. It has wavy wool and is very white and clear. It is 5¼ inches long.

Chow Dog Cover—A Chow dog rests on the cover of a split rib base. It is hard to find. A 5½ inch piece.

White Cat Cover—A cat rests on the cover of a coarse rib base. It is 5½ inches long.

Chow Dog Cover   White Cat Cover

PLATE 317

White Dog Top   White Dog. With Blue Head

PLATE 318

Walking Bear   White Cat Cover

PLATE 319

White Head Dog, Top—A dog with white head on a coarse rib base and it is a 5½ inch covered dish.

White Dog With Blue Head—A piece similar to the above but with a blue head. It is a 5¼ inch piece. These pieces have varying color schemes.

Walking Bear—A large 8 inch bear in a walking posture. It is a covered piece of British manufacture. Modern.

White Cat Cover—A 5½ inch dish with a white cat as a cover. It is a McKee piece and is much scarcer than the ordinary white cat pieces. A split rib base.

Frog Cover—A large frog rests on the cover of a 5½ inch dish, and a split rib base. It is rare. It is a Greentown, Ind., product.

Hen And Chickens—A small hen covered dish in which there are several small chick heads protruding. It is a basket weave base.

Frog Cover   Hen And Chicken

PLATE 320

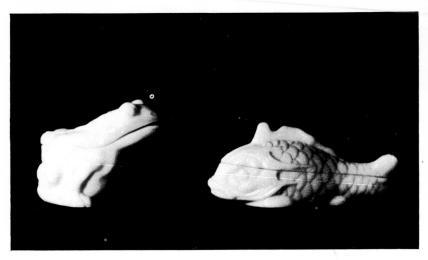

Sitting Frog

PLATE 321

Vallerystall Fish Covered

Rabbit On Wheat Base

PLATE 322

Jack Rabbit

Sitting Frog—A large frog in a sitting posture with mouth slightly open. It has a cover which is part of the body. It is modern.

Vallerystall Fish, Covered—A large fish shaped dish made by the French. The lid forms a part of the body.

Rabbit On Wheat Base—A leaping rabbit among vegetation rests on a base showing harvest scene. It is a Flaccus piece.

Jack Rabbit—A large squatting rabbit with ears lain on its body. It is properly on a fine rib base. It is a Flaccus piece.

Small Hen On Basket—Here is a small hen setting on a small basket which is handled. A Westmorland piece.

Chicks On Basket—A cluster of small chicks are on a small basket.

Emerging Chick On Basket—A chick is emerging from an egg on a small handled basket. It was made by The Westmorland Co., at Grapeville, Pa.

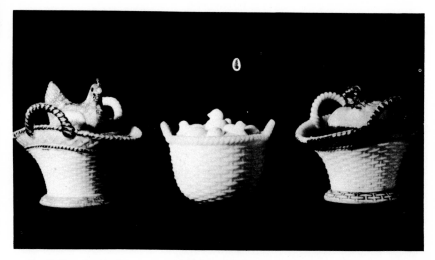

Small Hen On Basket   Chicks On Basket   Emerging Chick On Basket

PLATE 323

White Wagon   Automobile   Empty Sleigh

PLATE 324

Dominecker Hen and Rooster

PLATE 325

White Wagon—A small white trinket in the shape of a wagon.

Automobile—A white piece representing an automobile, and like its predecessor is a trinket.

Empty Sleigh—Here is the usual 5½ inch sleigh with nothing in it.

Dominecker Rooster And Hen—A pair of large 8 inch hen and rooster which have been painted to represent dominecker chickens. There are artificial eyes in most of these colored chickens. They vary considerably in the color scheme. They both, properly rest on a large basket base. They are Atterbury pieces.

GLOSSARY

A

A.B.C. Plate, Plate 47.
Acorn Overlay Vase, Plate 194.
Actress Head Bottle, Plate 141.
American Hen, Plate 296
American Skillet, Plate 69
Anchor And Belaying Pin Plate, Plate 42.
Anchor And Yacht Plate, Plate 28.
Ancient Castle Plate, Plate 23.
Angel And Harp Plate, Plate 13.
Angel Head Plate, Plate 5.
Anvil Salt, Plate 169.
Apple Blossom Covered Sugar, Plate 215.
Apple Blossom Jar, Plate 113.
Apple Blossom Salt, Plate 166.
Arch Border Compote, Plate 80.
Arch Border Plate, Plate 1.
Arch Edged Fruit Dish, Plate 135.
Ash Tray, Three Monks, Plate 57.
Automobile, Plate 324.

B

Backward "C" Plate, Plate 4.
Ball And Chain Edge Compote, Plate 87.
Barber Bay Rum Bottle, Plate 84C.
Bar And Swirl Mug, Plate 195.
Barred Hobnail Compote, Plate 75.
Barred Hobnail Sauce, Plate 75.
Basket Base Duck, Plate 272.
Basket Match Holder, Plate 248A.
Basket Sauce, Handled, Plate 183.
Basket, Scroll, Plate 196.
Basket Toothpick Holder, Plate 248A.
Basket Weave Compote, Plate 121.
Basket Weave Egg Cup, Plate 194.
Basket Weave Salt, Plate 172.
Basket Weave Tumbler, Plate 210.
Basket With Chicks, Square, Plate 314.
Battle Ship Maine, Plate 300.
Battle Ship Maine Plate, Plate 41.
Battle Ship, Uncle Sam, Plate 309.
Bay Rum Bottle, Plate 139.
Bay Rum Bottle, Tall, Plate 109.
Beaded Band Cruet, Plate 113.
Beaded Belt Match Holder, Plate 159.
Beaded Bottom Salt, Plate 160.
Beaded Bulb Lamp, Plate 264.
Beaded Circle Milk Pitcher, Plate 141.
Beaded Edge Dish, Plate 30.

Beaded Edge Nappie, Plate 49.
Beaded Edge, Square Dish, Plate 63.
Beaded Handle Mug, Plate 203.
Beaded Jewel Creamer, Plate 153.
Beaded Loop Indian Head Plate, Plate 12.
Beaded Loop Lamp, Plate 249.
Beaded Loop Lamp, No Flue, Blue. Plate 252.
Beaded Loop Vase, Marble Glass, Plate 230.
Beaded Match Holder, Plate 196.
Beaded Medallion Footed Nappie, Plate 95.
Beaded Medallion Lamp, Plate 248.
Beaded Medallion Mug, Plate 82.
Beaded Panel Salt, Plate 163.
Beaded Panel Syrup, Plate 126.
Beaded Rib Bowl, Plate 73.
Beaded Rib Open Slatted Compote, Plate 92.
Beaded Rib Tumbler, Plate 132.
Beaded Scroll Syrup, Plate 128.
Beaded Top Kettle, Plate 164.
Beaded Tumbler, Marble Glass, Plate 224.
Bear, Standing, Plate 282.
Bear, Three, Plate, Plate 16.
Bear, Walking, Plate 319.
Beaver Covered Dish, Plate 314.
Bee Hive Sugar, Plate 134.
Bee Match Holder, Black, Plate 236.
Bellflower Syrup, Plate 130.
Bible Match Holder, Plate 222.
Bird Shaped Pickle, Plate 135.
Black Bee Match Holder, Plate 236.
Blackberry Compote, Plate 118.
Blackberry Egg Cup, Plate 192.
Blackberry Footed Sauce, Plate 196.
Blackberry Spooner, Plate 155.
Blackberry Sugar, Plate 118.
Black Hen, Plate 274.
Black Hen, White Head, Plate 274.
Black Leaf Border Plate, Plate 40.
Black, Square "S", Plate, Plate 40.
Black Tumbler, Marble Glass, Plate 230.
Black Turtle, Plate 236.
Block and Circle Lamp, Plate 252.
Block and Fan Creamer, Plate 153.
Block and Jewel Mug, Plate 82.
Block and Oval Sauce, Plate 195.
Block Border, Notched Plate, Plate 7.
Block Border Plate, Plate 5.
Block Border Sauce, Plate 183.
Block Border, Square Plate, Plate 8.

Block Lamp, Plate 253.
Blue Duck, Plate 291.
Blue Head Hen, Lacy Edge Dish, Plate 267.
Blue Hen and Rooster, Plate 275.
Blue Marble Glass Hen, Lacy Edge Dish, Plate 269.
Boar Head, Plate 268.
Boat Nappie, Sunflower, Plate 91.
Boat Salt, Plate 197.
Boat Salt, Sandwich Plate 97.
Boat Salt, Scalloped Edge, Plate 198.
Book Match Holder, Plate 201.
Boot, Marble Glass, Plate 199.
Bo Peep Platter, Little, Plate 186.
Bottle, Actress Head, Plate 141.
Bottle, Bay Rum, Plate 139.
Bottle, Bulb Bottom, Plate 140.
Bottle, Bulb Neck, Plate 136.
Bottle, Bulging, Plain, Plate 299.
Bottle, Cologne, Plate 139.
Bottle, Draped Scroll, Plate 143.
Bottle, French Cologne, Plate 142.
Bottle, Gargoyle Head, Plate 143.
Bottle, Grant's Tomb, Plate 136.
Bottle, Hobnail, Plate 83.
Bottle, Leaf, Plate 145.
Bottle, Long Neck, Plate 136.
Bottle, Pansy, Plate 218.
Bottle, Ring Handle, Plate 136.
Bottle, Sawtooth, Covered, Plate 149.
Bottle, Scroll Bottom, Plate 144.
Bottle, Scroll Footed, Plate 141.
Bottle, Wich Hazel, Plate 140.
Bottle, Wide Lipped, Plate 144.
Bottle, Wreath Scroll, Covered, Plate 138.
Boudoir Lamp, Plain, Plate 265.
Bowl, Beaded Rib, Plate 73.
Bowl, Creased, Marble Glass, Plate 231.
Bowl, Crimped Edge, Plate 103.
Bowl, Draped Rib, Plate 72.
Bowl, Heavy Footed, Marble Glass, Plate 234.
Bowl, Hobnail, Plate 72.
Bowl, Hobnail, Pink Lined, Plate 84.
Bowl, Lacy Edged, Plate 205.
Bowl, Leaf Footed, Plate 103.
Bowl, Plain, Plate 72.
Box, Open Footed, Plate 191.
British Lion, Plate 308.
Brown Marble Glass Hen, Lacy Edge Dish, Plate 267.
Bryan Plate, Plate 50.
Bulb Bottom Vase, Plate 299.
Bulb Mustard, Plate 158.
Bulb Neck Bottle, Plate 136.
Bulb Whale Oil Lamp, Plate 252.
Bulbed Pot Lamp, Plate 253.
Bulbed Scroll Lamp, Plate 250.
Bulge Bottom Salt, Plate 160.
Bulging Vase, Plate 84C.

Bull Rushes, Moses In The, Plate 286.
Bull's Head Mustard, Plate 298.
Butter, Cross Fern, Plate 205.
Butter, Herringbone, Plate, 204.
Butter, Jacob's Coat, Plate 133.
Butter, Marble Glass, Fluted, Plate 224.
Butter, Roman Cross, Plate 75.
Butter, Sawtooth, Plate 211.
Butter, Tulip, Plate 135.
Butterfly Egg Cup, Plate 192.
Butterfly Match Holder, Plate 181.

C

"C", Backward, Plate 4.
"C", Double, Plate, Plate 19.
Cactus Coffee Urn, Caramel, Plate 242.
Cactus Mug, Caramel, Plate 241.
Cactus Pepper, Caramel, Plate 242.
Cactus Salt, Plate 165.
Cactus Salt, Caramel, Plate 242.
Cactus Tumbler, Caramel, Plate 241.
Cake Salver, Crimped Edge, Plate 74.
Cake Salver, Lacy Edge, Plate 74.
Cake Salver, Leaf Edge, Plate 49.
Cake Salver, Square, Plate 88.
Cake Stand, Fluted, Plate 125.
Cake Stand, Lattice Edge, Plate 117.
Cake Stand, Plain Ring Footed, Plate 125.
Camel, Lying, Plate 315.
Candle Holder, Footed, Plate 185.
Candle Holder, Palm and Bull's Eye, Plate 173.
Candle Holder, Pyramid, Plate 173.
Candle Holder, Sacred Crucifix, Plate 138.
Candle Holder, Saucer, Plate 185.
Candle Holder, Square, Plate 257.
Candle Holder, Square Foot, Plate 112.
Candle Holder, World's Fair, Plate 172.
Candle Sticks, Crucifix, Plate 177.
Candle Sticks, Ribbed Swirl, Plate 184.
Candle Sticks, Sandwich Dolphin, Plate 176.
Candy Stripe Lamp, Plate 266.
Cannon, Kettle Drum, Plate 301.
Cannon, Snare Drum, Plate 301.
Caramel Beaded Rib Mug, Plate 240.
Caramel Cactus Coffee Urn, Plate 242.
Caramel Cactus Mug, Plate 241.
Caramel Cactus Pepper, Plate 242.
Caramel Cactus Salt, Plate 242.
Caramel Cactus Sauce, Plate 239.
Caramel Cactus Tumbler, Plate 241.

Fern And Scroll Syrup, Plate 131.
Fern Spooner, Panelled, Plate 208.
Fish Cover, Plate 280.
Fish Covered Dish, Plate 289.
Fish, Covered, Valerystall, Plate
  321.
Fish Pickle Dish, Plate 68.
Fish Pickle, Waffle Type, Plate 308.
Fish Platter, Plate 67.
Fish Tray, Plate 54.
Five Loop Dresser Tray, Plate 84B
Flare Bottom Lamp, Plate 256.
Flared Lattice Compote, Plate 123.
Flask, Dog Head, Plate 112.
Flask, Fluted, Plate 139.
Flask, Klondyke, Plate 179.
Flask, Pipe And Bowl, Plate 137.
Flat Eared Rabbit, Plate 312.
Fleur de Lis Border Plate, Plate 15.
Fleur de Lis Flag, and Eagles
  Plate, Plate 32.
Fleur de Lis Lamp, Plate 250.
Fluer de Lis Match Holder, Plate
  248A.
Flower Border Plate, Plate 29.
Flower Compote, Panelled, Plate 122.
Flower Mug, Marble Glass,
  Plate 232.
Flower Salt, Panelled, Plate 161.
Flowered Sugar Shaker, Plate 94.
Flower Sugar Shaker, Plate 112.
Flower Vases, Panelled, Plate 110.
Flowered Vase, Plate 106.
Flute Salt, Plate 163.
Flute Sauce, Plate 203.
Fluted Cake Stand, Plate 125.
Fluted Compote, Plate 115.
Fluted Dresser Box, Plate 102.
Fluted Flask, Plate 139.
Fluted Mug, Plate 190.
Fluted Tumbler, Ribbed, Plate 193.
Fluted Vase, Plate 111.
Flying Fish Salt, Plate 102.
Footed Candle Holder, Plate 185.
Footed Dish, Wreath, Plate 71.
Footed Long Dresser Box, Platee 100.
Footed Match Holder, Square,
  Plate 196.
Footed Open Box, Plate 191.
Footed Salt, Rib, Plate 163.
Footed Scroll Salt, Plate 166.
Forget-me-not Deep Plate, Plate 26.
Forget-me-not, Plain Yoke,
  Triple Row Plate, Plate 8.
Forget-me-not, Single Row, Plate,
  Plate 48.
Forget-me-not, Triple Row, Plate,
  Plate 3.
Frog Cover, Plate 320.
Frog Sitting, Plate 321.
Fruit, Wine, Plate 157.

G

Gargoyle Head Bottle, Plate 143.
Gargoyle Head Platter, Plate 55.
Goblet, Ivy In Snow, Plate 92.
Goblet, Round Bowl, Marble
  Glass, Plate 229.
Goose Salt, Plate 164.
Gothic Plate, Plate 20.
Graces, The Three, Platter, Plate 52.
Grant's Tomb Bottle, Plate 136.
Grape, Cream, Plate, Plate 36.
Grape Creamer, Raised, Plate 154.
Grape Handled Sugar, Plate 133.
Grape Leaf Nappie, Plate 69.
Grape Mug, Plate 186.
Grape, Ruffled Top, Nappie,
  Plate 209.
Grape Spooner, Plate 155.
Grape Sugar Shaker, Plate 187.
Grape Toureen, Plate 90.
Grape Tumbler, Plate 191.
Grape Water Pitcher, Plate 263.
Grass Base Duck, Plate 271.
Green Leaf Plate, Plate 45.
Green Overlay Lamp, Plate 261.
Green Swirl Tumbler, Marble
  Glass, Plate 235.
Guttate Salt, Plate 168.

H

Hair Box, Deep, Iris, Plate 103.
Hair Box, Hexagonal, Plate 101.
Hair Box, Leaf Covered, Plate 188.
Hair Box, Milady's, Plate 101.
Hair Box, Needle Point, Plate 99.
Hair Box, Open Top, Plate 99.
Hair Box, Rose, Covered, Plate 188.
Hair Dish, Heart Shaped,
  Covered, Plate 98.
Hair Dish, Scroll Foot, Plate 98.
Hair Dish, Wreath, Plate 99.
Hand And Dove, Plate 76.
Hand And Fan, Plate 175.
Hand And Fan Match Holders,
  Plate 182.
Hand Compote, Plate 115.
Hand Vase, Blue, Plate 108.
Hands, Double, With Grapes,
  Plate 175.
Handled Basket Salt, Plate 183.
Handled Candle Holder, Blue,
  Plate 129.
Handled Master Salt, Marble
  Glass, Plate 236.
Handled Match Holder, Marble
  Glass, Plate 236.
Handled Nappie, Plate 96.
Handled Platter, Ring, Plate 109.
Handled, Ring, Mug, Plate 290.
Handled Tray, Ring, Plate 57.
Hare Plate, Plate 30.

M

Pyramid Candle Holder, Plate 173.
Pyramid, Footed, Lamp, Plate 255.
Pyramid Hexagon Salt, Plate 167.
Pyramid Sundae, Pink, Plate 112.
Pyramid Syrup, Plate 128.
Pyramid Vase, Plate 108.

Q

Quail Cover, Plate 280.
Question Mark Tray, Plate 60.

R

Rabbit And Horse-shoe Plate, Plate 43.
Rabbit, Caramel Dome, Plate 239.
Rabbit Chariot Plate, Plate 17.
Rabbit, Dome, Plate 313.
Rabbit, Flat Eared, Plate 312.
Rabbit, Jack, Plate 322.
Rabbit, Mule Eared, Plate 312.
Rabbit On Wheat Base, Plate 322.
Rabbit Salt, Plate 171.
Raised Grape Creamer, Plate 154.
Ram, Ribbed Base, Plate 184.
Ray End Tray, Plate 64.
Retriever Platter, Plate 63.
Rib Beaded, Caramel Mug, Plate 240.
Rib Bowl, Draped, Plate 72.
Rib Edge Tray, Plate 53.
Rib Edged Tray, Plate 59.
Rib Footed Dish, Marble Glass, Plate 233.
Ribbed Base Duck, Plate 270.
Ribbed Base Ram, Plate 184.
Ribbed Compote, Plate 119.
Ribbed Covered Sugar, Plate 207.
Ribbed Diamond Covered Jar, Plate 92.
Ribbed Dish Lion, Plate 307.
Ribbed Fluted Tumbler, Plate 193.
Ribbed Lacy Edge, Covered Sugar, Plate 134.
Ribbed Mug, Plate 189.
Ribbed Salt, Plate 160.
Ribbed Shell Creamer, Plate 154.
Ribbed Stem Compote, Plate 122.
Ribbed Sugar Shaker, Plate 128.
Ribbed Swirl Candle Sticks, Blue, Plate 184.
Ring And Dot Border Plate, Plate 31.
Ring Footed Plain Egg Cup, Plate 105.
Ring Handle Bottle, Plate 136.
Ring Handle Match Holder, Marble Glass, Plate 233.
Ring Handled Mug, Plate 290.
Ring Handled Platter, Plate 109.
Ring Handled Tray, Plate 57.

Ring Handled Vase, Plate 263.
Ringed Flat Lamp, Plate 255.
Ringed Vase, Plate 84C.
Robed Santa Claus On Sleigh, Plate 282.
Robin On Nest Compote, Plate 120.
Robin On Pedestal Nest, Plate 289.
Rock Of Ages Platter, Plate 52.
Rolled Edge Nappie, Plate 78.
Rolled Edge Tray, Plate 50.
Rolled Edge With Pinks, Tray, Plate 36.
Roman Cross Butter, Plate 75.
Roman Key Lamp, Plate 250.
Rooster And Hen, Large, Plate 273.
Rooster And Hen, White, Plate 287.
Rooster And Hens Plate, Plate 18.
Rooster, Pedestal, Plate 285.
Rooster, Straight Back, Plate 276.
Rose Covered Hair Box, Plate 188.
Rose Covered Jar, Plate 114.
Rose Cup And Saucer, Plate 178.
Rose Lid Trinket Box, Plate 99.
Rose Overlay Vase, Plate 110.
Rose Scroll Lamp, Plate 254.
Rose Vase, Large, Frontis Piece.
Rose Vase, Small, Plate 104.
Roses And Poppies, Platter, Plate 33.
Ruffled Top, Overlay Vase, Plate 138.

S

"S" Plate, Square, Black, Plate 39.
"S" Plate, Triangular, Plate 35.
Sacred Crucifix Candle Holder, Plate 138.
Sailor Hat, Plate 181.
Salt Anvil, Plate 169.
Salt, Apple Blossom, Plate 166.
Salt, Basket Weave, Plate 172.
Salt, Beaded Bottom, Plate 160.
Salt, Beaded Panel, Plate 163.
Salt, Boat, Plate 197.
Salt, Bulge Bottom, Plate 160.
Salt, Cactus, Plate 165.
Salt, Caramel Cactus, Plate 242.
Salt, Chick, Plate 157.
Salt, Chick Head, Plate 198.
Salt, Chicken, Plate 170.
Salt, Corn, Plate 167.
Salt, Cotton Bale, Plate 171.
Salt, Creased, Plate 166.
Salt, Creased Bale, Plate 197.
Salt, Creased Neck, Plate 167.
Salt, Creased Scroll, Plate 162.
Salt, Dahlia, Plate 161.
Salt, Daisy, Plate 161.
Salt, Diamond Block, Plate 168.
Salt, Double Rib, Plate 167.
Salt, Draped Leaf, Plate 165.
Salt, Egg, Plate 159.
Salt, Flute, Plate 163.

Shaker, Sugar, Ribbed, Plate 128.
Shaker, Sugar, Swirl, Plate 172.
Shaker, Swirl Sugar, Plate 172.
Shallow Heart Tray, Plate 37.
Sheep, Dome, Cover, Plate 282.
Shell Footed Creamer, Plate 210.
Shell Mug, Plate 190.
Shell Nappie, Lacy Edge, Plate 183.
Shell Pattern Set, Plate 216.
Shell Sugar, Panelled, Plate 207.
Shell Tray, Plate 68.
Ship, Cruiser, Plate 300.
Short Peg Plate, Plate 14.
Single Loop Edge Nappie, Plate 95.
Sitting Frog, Plate 321.
Skillet, Plate 200.
Skillet, American, Plate 69.
Sleigh, Chick In Egg On, Plate 284.
Sleigh, Empty, Plate 324.
Sleigh, Hen On, Plate 283.
Sleigh, Robed Santa Claus On.
  Plate 282.
Sleigh, Santa Claus On, Plate 283.
Slipper, Checkered, Plate 199.
Slipper, Daisy And Button,
  Plate 199.
Slipper, Large, Plate 182.
Slipper, Plain, Plate 199.
Small Elephant, Plate 304.
Small Hen On Basket, Plate 323.
Small Rose Vase, Plate 104.
Snare Drum Cannon, Plate 301.
Soap Dish, Square, Marble Glass,
  Plate 231.
Spider-webb Lamp, Plate 248.
Spider-webb Salt, Plate 169.
Split Rib Mug, Plate 180.
Split Rib Tumbler, Plate 192.
Spooner, Blackberry, Plate 155.
Spooner, Crown Top, Marble Glass,
  Plate 226.
Spooner, Grape, Plate 155.
Spooner, Panelled Fern, Plate 208.
Spooner, Princess Feather, Plate 151.
Spooner, Sawtooth, Plate 212.
Spooner, Thumbprint, Plate 208.
Spring Meets Winter Plate, Plate 9.
Sprinkler, Plate 203.
Square Basket With Chicks, Plate
  314.
Square Block Border Plate, Plate 8.
Square Cake Salver, Plate 88.
Square Dish, Beaded Edge, Plate 63.
Square Foot Candle Holder, Plate
  112.
Square Footed Match Holder, Plate
  196.
Square Lacy Edge Dish, Plate 73.
Square Leaf Syrup, Plate 126.
Square Match Holder, Marble Glass,
  Plate 232.
Square Pansy And Chain Plate,
  Plate 2.

Square Peg Plate, Plate 14.
Square Peg Plate, Small, Plate 84B.
Square "S" Plate, Black, Plate 39.
Square "S" Plate, Black, Small,
  Plate 40.
Square Scroll Covered Jar, Plate
  148.
Square Scroll Salt, Plate 162.
Square Set, Marble Glass, Plate 225.
Squirrel Cover, Plate 311.
Stanchion Border Plate, Plate 6.
Stanchion Border Plate, Black, Plate
  40.
Stanchion Border Plate, Blue
  Plate 41.
Standing Bear, Plate 282.
Star Cut Compote, Plate 87.
Star Plate, Plate 19.
Star Tray, Plate 66.
Stein Covered, Plate 218.
Stein, Monk, Plate 193.
Straight Back Rooster, Plate 276.
Straight Sided, Plain Vase, Plate
  108.
Stippled Dahlia Syrup, Blue, Plate
  156.
Stippled Forget-me-not Celery, Plate
  213.
Stippled Forget-me-not Creamer,
  Plate 213.
Stippled Forget-me-not Tumbler
  Plate 213.
Strawberry Dish, Covered, Plate 204.
Strawberry Egg Cup, Plate 98.
Strawberry Open Vase, Plate 219.
Strawberry Syrup, Plate 131.
Sugar, Bee Hive, Plate 134.
Sugar, Cherry, Plate 290.
Sugar, Cosmos, Open, Plate 214.
Sugar, Covered Apple Blossoms,
  Plate 215.
Sugar, Covered Swan, Plate 215.
Sugar, Crown Covered, Plate 214.
Sugar, Crown Top, Marble Glass,
  Plate 226.
Sugar, Crown Top, Plate 206.
Sugar, Grape, Handled, Plate 133.
Sugar, Hexagon, Marble Glass,
  Plate 224.
Sugar, Ibsen, Plate 134.
Sugar, Ribbed, Lacy Edge, Covered,
  Plate 134.
Sugar, Ribbed, Covered, Plate 207.
Sugar, Scoop, Plate 179.
Sugar Shaker, Corn, Plate 126.
Sugar Shaker, Flower, Plate 112.
Sugar Shaker, Flowered, Plate 94.
Sugar Shaker, Grape, Plate 187.
Sugar Shaker, Plain, Plate 166.
Sugar Shaker, Ribbed, Plate 128.
Sugar Shaker, Swirl, Plate 172.
Sugar, Shell, Panelled, Plate 207.